ARAB
ECONOMIC
INTEGRATION

ARAB ECONOMIC INTEGRATION

Between Hope and Reality

AHMED GALAL

BERNARD HOEKMAN

editors

EGYPTIAN CENTER FOR ECONOMIC STUDIES
Cairo

BROOKINGS INSTITUTION PRESS
Washington, D.C.

Arab Economic Integration: Between Hope and Reality may be ordered from
BROOKINGS INSTITUTION PRESS
1775 Massachusetts Avenue, N.W.
Washington, D.C. 20036
Tel.: 1-800/275-1447 or 202/797-6258
Fax: 202/797-6004
www.brookings.edu

Library of Congress Cataloging-in-Publication data

Arab economic integration : between hope and reality / Ahmed Galal and
Bernard Hoekman, editors.
    p.   cm.
Includes bibliographical references and index.
   ISBN 0-8157-3031-4 (pbk. : alk. paper)
   1. Arab countries—Economic integration.   2. Arab cooperation.
I.Galal, Ahmed, 1948–   II. Hoekman, Bernard M., 1959–

HC498.A7192 2003
337.1'174927—dc21   2003000073

                9 8 7 6 5 4 3 2 1

The paper used in this publication meets minimum requirements of the
American National Standard for Information Sciences—Permanence of Paper
for Printed Library Materials: ANSI Z39.48-1992.

Typeset in Minion

Composition by R. Lynn Rivenbark
Macon, Georgia

Printed by R. R. Donnelly
Harrisonburg, Virginia

Contents

Preface

Fifty years of repeated attempts at implementing the Arab economic integration project have left the region largely with just that—a project. Why? Is the future likely to be any different? Can the Arab states draw on the EU experience? This volume offers answers to these questions. The research project on which it is based was initiated by the Egyptian Center for Economic Studies (ECES) in an attempt to unravel the mystery of the persistent gap between the hope for economic integration and the reality of the limited achievements to date. The ultimate goal is to offer policymakers an assessment of the merits and means of—and the obstacles to—pursuing the integration project in the future.

This book would not have been possible without the support and valuable contributions of many individuals. In particular, we would like to express our deep appreciation to the board of directors of ECES for approving the research project and to the authors of the chapters for their splendid contributions. We also acknowledge the constructive feedback and insights of the participants in the ECES conference on Arab economic integration that was held in Cairo in October 2001. We are especially thankful to Sultan Abu Ali, Hanaa Kheir El Din, Moustafa El Feki, Heba Handoussa, Mounir Abdel Nour, and Ali Soliman for discussing the papers. We are also grateful to Mahmood Ayub, Gamal El Din El Bayoumi, and Taher Helmy for moderating the sessions and making valuable interventions. We are indebted to

Osama El Baz, Ian Boag, Youssef Boutros Ghali, and Gamal Mubarak for their frank and insightful views in the closing session of the conference.

We also are grateful to several individuals and institutions for their invaluable support and contributions to the successful production of this book. A number of the chapters in this volume draw on work undertaken for background papers for a 2001 Council on Foreign Relations study group on trade policy options for the Middle East and North Africa. The financial support of the Council on Foreign Relations is gratefully acknowledged by Konan, Messerlin, and Zarrouk, as are helpful comments by Mustapha Nabli and Maurice Schiff. We particularly wish to thank Robert Faherty and Christopher Kelaher of the Brookings Institution Press for their role in making this volume a reality. Thanks also go to Eileen Hughes for careful editing of the manuscript, Tanjam Jacobson for her valuable editorial assistance, and Yasser Selim for initial editing and reading of the final proofs. Nada Massoud, Nihal El-Megharbel, Amal Refaat, Noha Sherif, and Amina Taha provided excellent research assistance. Eman Mohsen and other ECES staff did an outstanding job of organizing the Cairo conference.

Finally, although many contributed to the publication of this volume, we take full responsibility for any errors or oversights.

AHMED GALAL
BERNARD HOEKMAN

ARAB
ECONOMIC
INTEGRATION

1

Between Hope and Reality:
An Overview of Arab Economic Integration

AHMED GALAL
BERNARD HOEKMAN

A rab economic integration (AEI) has been on the agenda of Arab politicians and intellectuals and of interest to the Arab public at large for some fifty years. The force behind AEI has been the widely held belief that the formation of a united Arab economic bloc would strengthen the bargaining power of the region in an increasingly polarized world and offer its people the opportunity to achieve a better standard of living. During this period, several attempts at economic integration have been made. The Arab League, for example, was created in 1945, providing a potential institutional means of carrying out such a project.

Fifty years later, however, AEI remains elusive, in contrast with the European economic integration experiment, which began around the same time. European Community members succeeded in converting their vision into reality, while supporters of AEI remain hopeful. The divergence in the outcomes of the two experiments raises a host of questions. Were the expected economic gains from AEI so small as to preclude taking concrete and systematic actions toward integration, or was it the absence of political incentives? Did the region lack the institutional mechanisms to carry out the project, or was it opposition from interest groups within individual countries

1

that has prevented real progress to date? Looking ahead, what is the possible impact of AEI on the welfare of the Arab countries involved? Are there any lessons to be drawn from the European Union (EU) experience for the Arab region, or are the two experiments so different that AEI must follow a unique path? These are the broad questions addressed in this volume.

The search for answers to these questions is now more pressing for the Arab region than ever before. Global competition has become more intense. International markets are increasingly dominated by regional economic powers. Economic progress in the developing world is quite uneven, with openness to trade being a feature of successful countries. In contrast and despite significant policy reform in the 1990s, the Arab countries remain less integrated among themselves than hoped for and less open to trade with the rest of the world than rapidly growing economies, and they still lag behind in economic performance. It is noteworthy, for example, that Egypt's per capita income, which in the 1950s was similar to that of Korea, today is less than one-fifth of Korea's. Morocco's per capita GDP, which was close to that of Malaysia, today is only one-third of Malaysia's. And Saudi Arabia's per capita GDP, which was higher than Taiwan's, now is only half.[1] Absent profound policy changes, GDP growth is not expected to exceed 3 to 4 percent in the coming decade. Given average growth in the labor force of more than 3 percent a year, it would be difficult to significantly reduce current levels of unemployment, which run as high as 20 percent in some countries.[2] The most recent *Arab Human Development Report* reaches a similar conclusion.[3] Despite significant progress in the region, much remains to be done to close the gap with most of the world on various human development indicators.

In this volume there is no presumption that Arab economic integration would necessarily improve the welfare of member countries, collectively or individually. Furthermore, there are no prior views on how to implement it. Rather, the focus is on addressing a number of key questions objectively, with a view to recommending a course of action. The analysis presented here complements previous work on regional integration carried out by the

---

1. Hoekman and Messerlin (2001).
2. Nabli and De Kleine (2000).
3. United Nations Development Program and Arab Fund for Economic and Social Development (2002).

Egyptian Center for Economic Studies (ECES) involving free trade agreements between a number of Arab countries and the EU[4] and the prospects of a free trade agreement between Egypt and the United States.[5]

In the chapters that follow, the authors provide an explanation of the outcomes of past efforts at Arab regional economic integration; offer an estimation of the expected benefits, should such integration be carried out; and discuss the possible lessons of the EU experience for the Arab region. Their objective is to identify the necessary preconditions for successful integration in the future.

Why Past Attempts at Arab Economic Integration Failed

Arab governments have a long history of negotiating regional trade agreements of many types, from bilateral treaties to reduce tariffs on a limited number of goods to ambitious programs aimed at creating an Arab common market. Most of these agreements have not been effective, and many were never fully implemented, resulting in limited intraregional trade compared with that of other regions (see chapter 2, table 2-1). Examples include a 1953 treaty to organize the transit of goods trade among the states of the Arab League; a 1964 agreement between Egypt, Iraq, Jordan, and Syria to establish an Arab common market; a 1981 agreement to facilitate and promote intra-Arab trade signed by eighteen member states of the Arab League; the short-lived Arab Cooperation Council, made up of Egypt, Iraq, Jordan, and Yemen; and the Maghreb Arab Union, composed of Algeria, Libya, Mauritania, Morocco, and Tunisia.[6]

To economists, nondiscriminatory liberalization of trade is preferable to regional economic integration agreements, as the latter can be costly in economic terms because of trade diversion. But regional agreements are not merely about economics. They typically have political objectives, and political gains may offset or outweigh economic costs. While it is difficult to attach the appropriate weight to each side of the equation, the challenge is to ensure that regional integration results in the attainment of overall net gains. Furthermore, it is important to realize that political gains tend to

4. Galal and Hoekman (1997).
5. Galal and Lawrence (1998).
6. Zarrouk (2000).

diminish over time as primary objectives are realized. Thus, even if the economic costs and benefits remain constant, continuous initiatives are needed to make up for the declining value of political gains.[7] The inability of regional integration arrangements to attain and maintain a positive overall cost-benefit balance may be why many agreements were stillborn or later died.

Was the lack of such balance responsible for the limited progress on AEI? In chapter 2, Fawzy suggests that political and economic incentives have been lacking. On the political front, concerns over the distribution of gains from integration across and within countries; national sovereignty; and the cost of adjusting to increased competition all constrained AEI. Shortage of "commitment" institutions, especially of mechanisms to compensate those who lose as a result of trade reform, and lack of consensus on choosing one or more states to act as regional leader were other limiting factors. On the economic front, Arab countries have not had sufficient incentives to integrate because they have had similar production structures, sheltered by high levels of protection. One consequence of this has been limited intra-Arab trade.[8] Further, because they have had less hospitable investment environments, higher transaction costs, and more restrictive barriers to entry than comparable countries, intraregional investment also has been limited.

Have the significant reforms of the last two decades changed the economic incentives sufficiently to favor AEI? Only partially. Both the incentives offered to firms and nontariff barriers continue to deter Arab intraregional trade and investment. Galal and Fawzy show in chapter 3 that in Egypt the prevailing incentive structure continues to favor production for the domestic market. Their conclusion is based on a simple simulation of the profitability of two Egyptian firms that are identical in all respects, except that one of them faces the incentive structure of an export company and the other the incentive structure of a company that produces for domestic consumption. It is based also on a simulation of the profitability of an Egyptian exporter compared with that of a similar exporter in other developing countries. This anti-export bias, which originates from an over-

7. Messerlin (2001).

8. This point is explored in depth in chapter 6 in this volume and elsewhere by Al-Atrash and Yousef (2000), Devlin and Page (2001), Havrylyshyn and Kunzel (2000), and Yeats and Ng (2000).

valued exchange rate, high tariff levels, and high interest and corporate tax rates, persists even when the partial compensation of exporters through duty and tax exemptions is taken into account. This means that trade liberalization has not gone far enough to reverse decades of inward-looking industrialization strategies, and most Egyptian firms still do not find it attractive to export to other Arab countries or to the rest of the world. Considering that a similar bias might exist in other Arab nations, it is not surprising that regional integration has been limited.

In chapter 4, Zarrouk estimates the magnitude and incidence of nontariff barriers for eight Arab countries on the basis of a survey of the private sector. The results indicate that the cost of compliance with all non–tariff-related measures averages 10 percent of the value of goods shipped. Next to bureaucratic red tape, customs clearance procedures are the most important source of nontariff trading costs. The average company spends ninety-five workdays a year resolving problems with customs and other government authorities. On average, unofficial payments associated with customs clearance account for only 1 percent of the value of shipments, but one-fifth of survey respondents reported paying between 2 and 17 percent.[9] Excessive delays result from the lengthy inspection and clearance process, the number of documents and signatures needed to process a trade transaction, and frequent problems with customs and other government authorities.

The 1998 Greater Arab Free Trade Area (GAFTA) agreement will not entirely reduce or eliminate these nontariff barriers. It is true that, unlike previous attempts, GAFTA embodies specific commitments requiring across-the-board elimination of tariffs, tariff-like charges, and nontariff measures.[10] Import duties and other barriers to trade in goods of Arab origin are to be eliminated by 2008. However, GAFTA is a traditional (shallow) preferential trade agreement, limited to trade in merchandise. Services and investment are excluded, greatly reducing the agreement's ability to exert a significant positive economic impact. As a result, nontariff measures are likely to remain important barriers to regional integration, unless further reforms are undertaken.

9. The survey indicates that a number of Arab countries, such as Egypt and Jordan, have improved the performance of customs in recent years. In other countries, such as Lebanon, Saudi Arabia, and Syria, matters either have not improved or have deteriorated.

10. Zarrouk (2000).

Whatever the obstacles to AEI in the past, whether the project is likely to be beneficial is the key question determining political incentives to integrate. This question is taken up in chapter 5.

The Likely Impact of Arab Economic Integration

Ideally, a general equilibrium model for each country affected is needed to answer the question of whether AEI would be beneficial. The changes that AEI would bring could then be introduced to determine the likely impact for each country and for the region as a whole. Given that economic integration could take the form of shallow integration (involving only reforms of policies applied at national borders) or deep integration (involving additional "behind the border" reforms), different simulations would have to be carried out under various assumptions.

Although an assessment of the likely impact of AEI on all Arab countries is not available, in chapter 5 Konan provides such an estimate for Egypt and Tunisia, using an economywide model for each country. Simulations were carried out for both shallow and deep forms of integration, focusing in particular on the impact of improving the efficiency of service industries (for example, finance, transportation, marketing) in light of their importance to the competitiveness of Arab firms.[11] Although the exact numbers differ for Egypt and Tunisia, the qualitative results are remarkably similar. The most significant result is that comprehensive service sector reforms would generate gains far superior to those that could be attained through tariff removal alone. Overall, gains estimated at 13 percent of GDP for Tunisia and 10 percent for Egypt could be attained through competition and reform of regulations governing the service sector. In the case of Tunisia, the estimated gains are more than three times those that would be generated by the liberalization of trade in merchandise alone; for Egypt, the gains are double. The reasons why deeper reforms that improve the efficiency of the service sector would improve welfare significantly are not difficult to grasp. Reforming

---

11. Recent ECES studies illustrate the importance of efficient services to the economy. Mansour (2001) identifies the services most needed to support the competitiveness of small and medium enterprises (SMEs) in a sample of Arab countries. Tohamy (2001) discusses the importance of services generally and documents the extent of service sector liberalization in Egypt. Galal (1999) estimates the potential gains from greater competition and deregulation in the Egyptian telecommunications sector.

the service sector affects the economy as a whole, not just the external sector; it entails removing high barriers to entry for both domestic and foreign firms; and it eliminates policies that create needless transaction costs. This differs from merchandize trade liberalization, which gives rise to efficiency gains only.

This does not mean that liberalizing trade in merchandise should be stopped or postponed. Gains are highest if both reform agendas are pursued. Trade liberalization aligns domestic and world prices, and price alignment is a critical factor in ensuring that investments are allocated efficiently, materials are obtained from the least costly suppliers, and firms have access to the latest technologies. Trade liberalization also is key to reducing the cost of adjustment to reform. Scenarios in which governments eliminate domestic distortions first and then turn to border distortions (trade barriers) produce unfavorable results. That approach not only reduces real income gains, it also exacerbates adjustment costs. Labor has to undergo "churning" from one sector to another. During the initial stage, domestic resources would flow to the most protected industrial and service sectors. Subsequent service sector reforms would generate shifts in the opposite direction.

In sum, the likely economic impact of AEI is positive, at least for Egypt and Tunisia. Gains are expected to be much greater if AEI involves actions to increase the efficiency of the service sector as well as the removal of tariff and nontariff barriers to trade. Whether similar gains can be expected for other Arab countries, especially oil-producing nations, remains an open question. Assuming that the net gains are positive for the majority of participating countries, the question arises as to the nature and optimal path for making progress on AEI. Chapters 6 and 7 look for clues from the EU experience.

Lessons from the EU

In many respects, understanding the experience of the EU is highly relevant to understanding past Arab regional integration efforts and to informing future attempts. Both the EU and earlier AEI experiments were politically motivated. Both sought to use economic cooperation as a mechanism for integration. Proximity was another common factor. For those reasons, it is instructive to look at the EU experience for insights, keeping in mind the

historical context of the two regions, the initial condition of their economies, and the structure of economic incentives. Another major reason for
looking at the EU experience is that it is the preeminent example of successful integration.

Although the two regions have similarities, their differences seem to be
much larger. In chapter 6, Hoekman and Messerlin show that the conditions
that prevailed in the 1950s and 1960s in Europe are quite different from
those prevailing in the Arab region today. Differences in size, level of development, market structure, and level of protection all suggest that regional
liberalization of trade in goods is not likely to be the best way to integrate
Arab countries. Instead, simultaneous action involving nondiscriminatory
trade liberalization and concerted reform of service markets may be more
successful.[12]

Why would such a strategy have a better chance of success in the Arab
region? The answer lies in the political constraints on trade policy reforms,
especially when trade barriers are high and costly, as they are in the Arab
economies. Trade policy is about a set of domestic bargains between conflicting domestic interests. Some gain, some lose. For liberalization and integration to succeed, there must be a sufficiently large domestic coalition that
favors it over all alternatives, including the status quo.[13] Given the high level
of trade protection in the Arab region, building such a coalition is critical,
but it is difficult. In contrast, because services are a major input into the
production process as well as activities such as distribution and sales, liberalization of services could generate significant gains from lower costs of
production for the manufacturing and agricultural sectors—each a large
and powerful constituency. Reductions in those costs should facilitate trade
liberalization by enhancing the competitiveness of industry and agriculture.
In addition, service sector reforms would increase investment in the liberal-

---

12. Hoekman and Messerlin further note, without elaboration, that integration of factor
markets could complement a services-based integration strategy. Trade in labor traditionally
has been relatively large in the Arab region—probably more so than in the EU. In fact, factor
mobility and trade in services may have been a substitute for trade in goods in the Arab
region, where there was significant labor mobility from labor-abundant countries (for example, Egypt, Jordan, and Lebanon) to labor-scarce countries (for example, Saudi Arabia and
Kuwait). However, lack of cooperative arrangements may have constrained labor mobility so
that it was less than it might have been. An agreement on a more stable and well-anchored
regime of labor movement within the region could have significant payoffs.
13. Galal (2000).

ized industries, which would generate employment opportunities for skilled and unskilled workers employed by government or import-competing industries or for those who are unemployed. While the deregulation of entry will inevitably result in the restructuring of domestic industry, service sector reform has less far-reaching implications for sectoral turnover and aggregate employment than the abolition of trade barriers because services often need to be consumed where they are produced.[14]

In chapter 7, Winters identifies the key institutional features that made the EU integration effort a success. From the outset, the project was seen as a whole and as a process, rather than as a series of separate steps. There was strong political backing for integration and a central executive body to manage the process and push it forward. The grand vision of integration provided the basis for what followed, while the European Commission acted as guardian of the integration ideal during times of recession. Mechanisms for redistribution were devised to sustain cooperation, as was an agreement to pursue integration gradually.

The Way Forward

Perhaps the most important step on the road to AEI is to acknowledge the glaring fact that fifty years later, it remains more of a hope than a reality. No matter how well-intentioned past efforts have been, they have not been effective. Accordingly, a choice has to be made among three broad options: abandoning the AEI project altogether, continuing business as usual on the basis of preferential trade liberalization, or taking a leap forward by capitalizing on the experience to date. The choice must be informed by political, not just economic, factors. Abandoning the AEI project altogether means forgoing potentially significant gains to the region. The second option is highly imperfect, since preferential trade liberalization was met with strong resistance in the past and is in any event unlikely to be very beneficial. The most viable option is to capitalize on the lessons of experience to devise an alternative, more ambitious path to integration in the future, one that has clear economic payoffs.

If a more ambitious approach to AEI is chosen, the next step is to develop a common vision about the ultimate form of integration, at least initially

---

14. Konan, chapter 5 of this volume.

among a small core group of countries. To the founders of the EU, it was clear that the objective of the union was to create a common market with a common external commercial policy and eventually to allow the free movement of goods, services, investment, and labor among member states. For the Arab region, it is important to clearly articulate an ultimate objective. Two options that stand out are to create either an Arab common market or a deeper free trade agreement that extends to cooperation on regulatory policies and common institutions. The choice between these options is fundamentally a political decision.

Once a vision is agreed upon, the next step is to select an appropriate path to achieve it. In the EU case, regional trade liberalization provided the basis for further integration. Mobility of labor, liberalization of foreign direct investment, and efforts to reduce the regulatory barriers that segmented national service markets were to follow. Indeed, serious efforts to liberalize trade and investment in services did not occur before the 1990s, through the European "single market" or "1992" initiative. The path followed in the Arab region also started with the liberalization of intra-Arab trade in goods, although subsequent steps have not been articulated. Given that labor is somewhat mobile in the Arab region and that service markets are relatively inefficient, an alternative path could emphasize parallel agreements on trade liberalization (as in GAFTA), labor mobility, and liberalization of services, which would have a noticeable impact on firm competitiveness. That is not to say that all actions on those three fronts have to be undertaken up front, but that simultaneous progress on all is desirable to enhance their impact. The merits of such an approach are twofold: it should generate significant economic gains and help mobilize support for further trade reform among workers, industrialists, and agriculturists.

Given the vision and the path, the next step is to rethink the institutions necessary to carry out an integration project. In the EU case, the structure included supranational institutions: an executive agency (the European Commission), a political oversight body (the European Council), a judiciary (the European Court of Justice), and a directly elected European Parliament. The design of the institutional arrangements for AEI has to take into account the nature of the agreed-upon project, existing institutions, and the gaps between both. Broadly speaking, if AEI remains a shallow form of integration focusing on regional liberalization of trade in goods, there is minimal need for adjustment of current institutional arrangements. On the other hand, if the project is redesigned to favor an Arab common market, implementation would require major institutional changes. The model in this case is analogous to that of the EU, and the lessons laid out by Winters in chapter 7 become highly relevant. If, in a third scenario midway between the two, a deeper form of regional economic integration is created that does not include a common external trade policy, a careful revision of existing institutions is necessary. While the results of such a revision cannot be judged beforehand, the likelihood is high that it would require strengthening an entity within the Arab League to oversee the design and enforcement of the broad issues of the agreement as well as creating new entities to address new areas of agreement—for example, labor mobility and liberalization of network services.

The project's timeframe and credibility both are crucial to its overall success. In particular, sufficient time should be allowed to enable countries to adjust at a pace that is socially acceptable to them. The more difficult task is to build credibility, especially in light of a history of fifty years of making agreements that do not stick. But here is where external commitments and political leadership make a real difference.

References

Al-Atrash, Hassan, and Tarik Yousef. 2000. "Intra-Arab Trade: Is It Too Little?" IMF Working Paper 00/10. Washington: International Monetary Fund (January).

Devlin, Julia, and John Page. 2001. "Testing the Waters: Arab Integration, Competitiveness, and the Euro-Med Agreements." In *Towards Arab and Euro-Med Regional Integration*, edited by Sebastien Dessus, Julia Devlin, and Raed Safadi. Paris: Organization for Economic Cooperation and Development.

Galal, Ahmed. 1999. "The Welfare Impact of Telecom Reform in Egypt: An Ex Ante Analysis." In *Partners for Development: New Roles for Government and the Private Sector in the Middle East and North Africa*, edited by Samiha Fawzy and Ahmed Galal. Washington: World Bank.

———. 2000. "Incentives for Economic Integration in the Middle East." In *Trade Policy Developments in the Middle East and North Africa*, edited by Bernard Hoekman and Hanaa Kheir-El-Din. Washington: World Bank.

Galal, Ahmed, and Bernard Hoekman, eds. 1997. *Regional Partners in Global Markets: Limits and Possibilities of the Euro-Med Agreements*. London: Center for Economic Policy Research.

Galal, Ahmed, and Robert Lawrence, eds. 1998. *Building Bridges: An Egypt-U.S. Free Trade Agreement*. Brookings.

Havrylyshyn, Oleh, and Peter Kunzel. 2000. "Intra-Industry Trade of Arab Countries: An Indicator of Potential Competitiveness." In *Catching Up with the Competition: Trade Opportunities and Challenges for Arab Countries,* edited by Bernard Hoekman and Jamel Zarrouk. University of Michigan Press.

Hoekman, Bernard, and Patrick Messerlin. 2001. *Harnessing Trade for Development in the Middle East and North Africa.* New York: Council on Foreign Relations.

Mansour, Antoine. 2001. "Support Services and the Competitiveness of SMEs in the Arab Region." ECES Working Paper No. 56. Cairo: Egyptian Center for Economic Studies (May).

Messerlin, Patrick. 2001. *Measuring the Costs of Protection in Europe.* Washington: Institute for International Economics.

Nabli, Mustapha, and Annette De Kleine. 2000. "Managing Global Integration in the Middle East and North Africa." In *Trade Policy Developments in the Middle East and North Africa.*

Tohamy, Sahar. 2001. "Case Study of Egypt's Service Liberalization, Service Barriers, and Implementation of the GATS." In *Services in the International Economy,* edited by R. Stern. University of Michigan Press.

United Nations Development Program and the Arab Fund for Economic and Social Development. 2002. *Arab Human Development Report.* New York.

Yeats, Alexander, and Francis Ng. 2000. "Beyond the Year 2000: Implications of the Middle East's Recent Trade Performance." In *Catching Up with the Competition.*

Zarrouk, Jamel. 2000. "The Greater Arab Free Trade Area: Limits and Possibilities." In *Catching Up with the Competition.*

2

The Economics and Politics
of Arab Economic Integration

SAMIHA FAWZY

> *The inability to mobilize the considerable collective human and*
> *material resources of a "nation" of more than 200 million people*
> *accounts in part for the powerlessness which is the fundamental*
> *problem facing the Arabs today.*
> —EDWARD SAID, 1996

A nyone who has a fair knowledge of the Arab region knows that the notion of pan-Arab unity has long been central to Arab culture and history. The Arabs also were among the pioneers calling for regional integration in the early 1950s. However, despite repeated attempts at regional integration over half a century, Arab economic relations remain limited and compare unfavorably with those of other regional blocs. While regionalism has gained momentum all over the world, Arab regional integration remains merely a "project." This state of affairs persists despite findings from a number of studies that show that integration among Arab countries could entail positive welfare gains.[1] It is important, therefore, to explore the reasons for the limited progress to date.

The views expressed in this chapter are those of the author and should not be attributed to the Egyptian Center for Economic Studies (ECES) or to Cairo University. The author would like to thank Nihal El-Megharbel of ECES for outstanding research assistance and Amina Taha of ECES for excellent support.
    1. Hoekman and others (1998); Galal and Hoekman (1997); Konan and Maskus (1997).

13

More specifically, this chapter addresses the following questions: What economic and political factors have stood in the way of integration up to now? How have other regions overcome similar problems? Finally, how can Arab countries ensure a more promising future for integration? To answer these questions, the chapter draws on the economic and political literature on regional integration. The main proposition underlying the analysis is that both economic and political incentives must exist if regional arrangements are to succeed. Because regional economic integration takes place in a particular political and institutional setting, any economic analysis of regional integration that ignores political and institutional elements risks becoming irrelevant. Similarly, a political analysis that omits the economics of regional integration is misleading. Without a multidisciplinary approach, the study may be ill defined and the analysis may lead to vague policy recommendations.[2]

Economic incentives are highlighted by standard customs union theory as well as more recent regional integration theory.[3] According to these theories, countries are motivated to integrate if integration enhances their welfare—in other words, if it is associated with static and dynamic gains. Political incentives may be driven by security or other concerns. In both cases, political leaders must show willingness to create the institutions necessary to sustain integration. It also is essential that they accept that one or more members of the group play the role of regional leader. Regional leadership can serve to coordinate rules and policies and may help ease distributional problems.[4]

In exploring the applicability of this theoretical framework to the Arab region, this chapter first reviews the track record of regional integration in the Arab world to date. It then discusses the extent to which economic and political incentives were aligned with the goals of Arab economic integration. Last, it explores future prospects for integration and offers some concluding remarks.

---

2. Escribano (2000); Mattli (2000).
3. Viner (1950); Lawrence (1997); De Melo and Panagariya (1993).
4. Haas (1968); Moravcisk (1991).

The Track Record

There has been no shortage of attempts by Arab countries to cooperate, form alliances, or achieve integration during the last five decades. However, little has been achieved so far. At the risk of oversimplification, it can be said that from the end of World War II to the late 1990s there were two distinct phases regarding attempts to encourage intra-Arab economic relations. The first was in the Arab postindependence period, which began after World War II; the second started with the oil boom in the early 1970s. During the first phase, three factors were behind integration efforts: the establishment of the Arab League in 1945; the UN efforts to promote regional coopera- tion; and the creation of the European Common Market in 1957. Early attempts at Arab regionalism included the Treaty for Joint Defense and Economic Cooperation in the early 1950s, followed in 1953 by the Convention for Facilitating Trade and Regulating Transit Trade and in 1957 by the Arab Economic Unity Agreement. In 1964, there were endeavors to create an Arab common market.

During this phase, efforts aimed at achieving regional integration relied mainly on trade promotion. While contributing to intra-Arab trade in the 1950s and 1960s, these efforts fell short of meeting the objectives of eco- nomic integration. It seems that Arab politicians focused more on political and military cooperation and did not pay enough attention to economics, considering business and commerce to be effects, not causes, of political action.[5]

The second phase, which started with the boom in oil prices in 1973, led to an increase in the flow of capital and labor within the region and, to a lesser extent, in intraregional trade. The increase in oil revenues coupled with the limited success of economic integration in the first phase prompted a search for alternative strategies. The first integration strategy in the 1970s sought to establish joint projects through the active involvement of govern- ments, but it soon became apparent that by itself this strategy would not achieve economic integration. This shortcoming gave rise to a strategy of economic integration at the subregional level. As a result, the 1980s saw the advent of the Gulf Cooperation Council (GCC), the Arab Cooperation

5. Sayigh (1999); Owen (1999).

Council (ACC), and the Arab Maghreb Union (AMU).[6] Some observers believed that subregional cooperation was more likely to succeed because it involved a smaller number of countries. However, despite the growth of intraregional trade within these subgroups, expansion was limited compared with growth in external trade. It has been argued that smaller subregional groupings may have been partially responsible for delaying the Arab integration project.[7]

Because subregional blocs did not help much in promoting intra-Arab trade, an attempt to revive Arab integration at the regional level was made in 1981 through the Agreement for Facilitation and Promotion of Intra-Arab Trade. This effort culminated in 1997 in a renewed interest in forming an Arab free trade area (AFTA). Eighteen Arab states joined the agreement, which went into effect on January 1, 1998. This program revived the 1981 agreement to facilitate and promote intra-Arab trade.[8] Notwithstanding these efforts, the outcomes have been negligible. Below is a brief review of the evolution of Arab economic relations in terms of trade and factor movements.

Intra-Arab Trade

Figure 2-1 shows that intra-Arab exports increased from 5.2 percent of total exports in 1970 to 8.2 percent in 1998. However, the average share of intra-Arab exports in total exports, nearly 7 percent, is far below the share of intraregional exports in other regions: 60 percent for the EU, 22 percent for the Association of Southeast Asian Nations (ASEAN), and 41 percent for parties to the North American Free Trade Agreement (NAFTA) (table 2-1). When oil exports are excluded, the average share of intra-Arab exports increased to 19 percent, a level that is still lower than that in the other regional blocs.

To judge whether intra-Arab trade is too limited, Al Atrash and Yousef used a gravity model to compare the actual and potential levels of trade.[9] Their study indicates that both actual intra-Arab trade and Arab exports to the rest of the world are lower than the model predicted, implying that the potential for trade is greater than the trade that is actually occurring. This finding does not hold across all industries. In fact, Havrylyshyn and Kunzel

6. El Naggar (1997).
7. Shafik (1994).
8. Zarrouk (1998).
9. Al-Atrash and Yousef (2000).

Figure 2-1. *Intra-Arab Exports and Non-Oil Intra-Arab Trade*

A: *Intra-Arab exports as a share of total exports*

B: *Non-oil intra-Arab exports as a share of non-oil total exports*

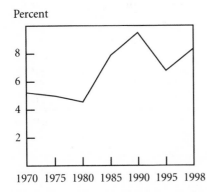

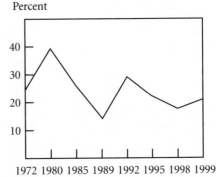

Sources: Panel A: International Monetary Fund, *Direction of Trade Statistics Yearbook,* 1997–2000. Panel B: Zarrouk (1992); Arab League (1999–2001).

and Devlin and Page showed that despite the low level of intraregional trade, some sectors—such as the chemical, iron, and steel industries—exhibit a high level of intra-industry trade.[10]

Capital Flows

Figure 2-2 shows that intra-Arab capital flows during the period from 1950 to 2000 were very modest, with the exception of the 1970s. Even when the peak period of capital flows in the 1970s is considered, capital flows amounted to only 2 percent of oil revenues. While oil revenues reached US$279 billion, the total amount of capital flows to the Arab countries did not exceed US$6 billion.[11]

The low level of intra-Arab capital flows can be traced to a number of factors. The nonexistence or underdevelopment of capital markets and prohibitive laws and regulations in the Arab world turned many Arab investors to international markets, which offered a better opportunity to maximize profitability and diversify risk. There also is evidence that excess capital in

10. Havrylyshyn and Kunzel (2000); Devlin and Page (2001).
11. In four Arab oil-exporting countries, Saudi Arabia, Kuwait, United Arab Emirates, and Qatar.

Table 2-1. *Intraregional Exports as a Percent of Total Exports, Selected Years*

Percent

Regional bloc	1970	1975	1980	1985	1990	1995	1998
AFTA	5.2	4.9	4.5	7.8	9.4	6.7	8.2
ASEAN	19.2	21.3	22.4	20.7	20.7	26.4	22.2
Mercosur	9	n.a.	12	6	9	20	25
APEC	58	n.a.	58	68	68	72	70
NAFTA	36	34.6	33.6	43.9	41.4	46.2	51
EU	59.5	57.7	60.8	59.2	65.9	62.4	56.8

Source: International Monetary Fund, *Direction of Trade Statistics Yearbook,* 1997–2000; World Bank, *World Development Indicators,* 2001 (CD-ROM).

the region was transferred to foreign banks and financial institutions, with a significant portion invested in gold and silver. El Erian and Fischer estimated Arab investment outside the region at US$350 billion to US$600 billion in 1995.[12]

Labor Mobility

Labor movement within the region has played a more significant role in intra-Arab economic exchange than intraregional trade, due in part to the fact that obstacles to labor flow have been less severe than those facing trade in goods. This also can be attributed in part to the wide difference in labor endowment across countries. Table 2-2, which displays workers' remittances as a percentage of GDP in selected countries, shows that Jordan, Yemen, Morocco, and Egypt are the biggest suppliers of labor in the region.

Clearly, immigration and its associated capital flows provided a mutually beneficial mechanism for sharing the region's oil wealth and for taking advantage of its underutilized human resources. However, labor movement did not work as a substitute for greater regional trade for three main reasons. First, labor in the Arab region does not enjoy the same degree of mobility found, for example, in the EU, where citizens of one country have the right to work in other countries. Second, the Gulf war and subsequent tensions among Arab countries have led to a reduction in the size of the Arab expatriate labor force and hence in remittances. Third, there has been

12. El Erian and Fischer (1996).

Figure 2-2. *Intra-Arab Private Capital Investment*

US$ billions

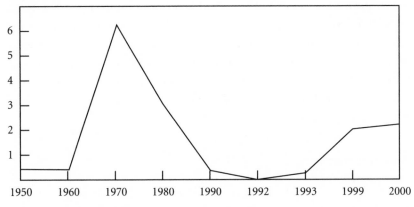

Source: Al-Monzery (1995).

a trend in oil-rich countries toward replacing Arab immigrants by nationals and cheap labor from Asia, thus weakening an important pillar of Arab integration.

To summarize, two observations can be drawn from the above analysis. First, the pattern of regional integration among Arab countries is quite unusual. In most parts of the world trade in goods forms the basis for regional integration, while labor mobility usually comes in the final stage. This was the pattern observed with the EU, ASEAN, and NAFTA. In contrast, intra-Arab trade has been limited, while labor movement has been the

Table 2-2. *Workers' Remittances as a Percent of GDP of the Main Regional Labor Suppliers*

Percent

Country	1975	1980	1985	1990	1995	1999
Algeria	n.a.	1	1	1	3	2
Egypt	3	12	10	9	5	4
Jordan	12	15	20	12	18	21
Morocco	6	6	8	8	6	6
Sudan	2	3	3	1	n.a.	n.a.
Tunisia	n.a.	4	3	4	4	4
Yemen	n.a.	n.a.	n.a.	32	27	18

Source: World Bank, *Global Development Finance*, 2001 (CD-ROM).

most visible element of Arab integration. Second, despite remarkable efforts to encourage economic integration among Arab states, the region remains one of the least integrated in the world in terms of capital and trade flows. Only labor has flowed relatively freely. It may be argued, therefore, that most past efforts seem to have focused more on drafting agreements and holding summits than on addressing the major barriers to Arab economic integration by trying to create the economic and political incentives necessary to achieve it. The next section deals with the economic factors behind the limited progress to date.

Economic Factors

Intuitively, one would expect the Arab world to have strong economic incentives to integrate in view of its rich and diverse factor endowment. The region encompasses 14 million square kilometers, almost equal in size to the EU and three-quarters the size of Latin America. It holds 5 percent of the world's population. Moreover, the distribution of labor, capital, and natural resources is quite uneven. Why then is there such a low level of integration?

The literature on economic incentives has evolved over time. When most countries were following import-substitution strategies with the twin features of protection and state domination, traditional customs union theory focused on the effects on trade promotion of removing tariff barriers, the so-called static gains. As explained by Viner, static gains depend on trade creation and trade diversion.[13] Trade creation refers to the new trade that can arise from substituting goods produced by neighbors for goods previously produced domestically. It implies a shift from a high-cost member of a bloc to a low-cost member and hence enhances welfare. Trade diversion refers to the shifting of existing trade from a low-cost nonmember to a high-cost member, which would have a negative effect on welfare. Obviously, the desirability of regional integration would depend on the net effect of trade creation and trade diversion.

In contrast, new explanations of regional integration have evolved at a time when most countries are following more open and outward-oriented strategies and when the private sector plays the leading role in economic activities. The development of incentives to integrate regionally resulted in

13. Viner (1950).

increased emphasis on the potential dynamic gains of integration, which are associated with increased investment, more competition, and improved productivity.[14]

The above gains are neither automatic nor instant. Certain conditions must be fulfilled to ensure that countries will benefit from regional arrangements and hence have sufficient motivation to integrate. On one hand, static gains are more likely when a regional bloc's member countries enjoy three conditions. First, their economies have a high degree of complementarity, which offers more room for trade creation. Second, the bloc includes many member countries, which means a larger market and greater opportunity for trade. Third, the countries enjoy geographical proximity, which reduces transportation costs and hence encourages trade. Although some argue that the telecommunications revolution reduces the importance of geographic proximity, it does not annul it.

On the other hand, benefiting from the dynamic gains of regional integration requires countries to be more open to trade, because the lower the tariff barriers, the more intense the competition, the larger the efficiency gains, the lesser the potential for trade diversion, and the weaker the opposition to integration. In addition, because a dynamic private sector increases the potential for trade promotion and for forming joint projects, the greater the role played by the private sector, the larger the likely gains. The question is whether Arab countries meet both sets of requirements.

Complementarity

Table 2-3 shows the complementarity index for each Arab country and the rest of the region, computed from data from the mid-1990s. The index measures how well different countries' import and export structures align. The index ranges from a value of zero, when goods not exported by one country are imported by another, to a value of 100, when the export and import shares are an exact match. The higher the value, the more likely regional integration is to succeed. Comparing the complementarity indexes for the Arab region to those of other regional blocs reveals a very low degree of complementarity among the trade structures of most Arab countries, which is unfavorable to intraregional trade. The same conclusion has been reached in several studies, which point out that the lack of complementarity among

---

14. Lawrence (1997); De Melo and Panagariya (1993).

Table 2-3. Trade Complementarity Indexes, 1990s

Regional arrangement	Index value
Successful	
European Community[a]	53.4
NAFTA	56.3
Unsuccessful	
Andean Pact	7.4
LAFTA	22.2
Arab countries[b]	
Bahrain	17.4
Egypt	28.0
Jordan	25.5
Kuwait	9.6
Lebanon	34.3
Libya	8.5
Oman	25.6
Qatar	13.6
Saudi Arabia	13.2
Syria	16.8
Yemen	5.9
UAE	20.6

Source: Yeats and Ng (2000).

a. Refers to the six original members.

b. Each entry refers to the complementarity between a given country and other Arab countries.

Arab countries was one of the main reasons for the limited trade gains from regional integration.[15]

It is worth mentioning that, according to the classical Heckscher-Ohlin model, the growth of intra-EU trade was driven not only by the high degree of complementarity among EU members that resulted from differences in their factor endowments; imperfect competition and product differentiation also played an important role.[16] That implies that even with the low level of complementarity among Arab states, intra-Arab trade can grow if they develop their industrial base, diversify, and specialize.

Large Number of Bloc Members

Despite the large number of Arab countries and the considerable size of their collective population (270 million), the Arab region's economic size is

15. Al-Atrash and Yousef (2000); Yeats and Ng (2000).
16. Shafik (1994).

limited, which may be one of the reasons for the limited progress of Arab integration. Furthermore, the wide differences in economic systems across countries impede deeper forms of economic relations even further.

More important, the divergence in the levels of development across countries works against deepening economic relations among Arab countries. The differences in per capita income in the region are more than twenty-one-fold, with Sudan having the lowest per capita income (US$610) and Kuwait the highest (US$12,710). The gaps are only tenfold and fivefold within NAFTA and the EU, respectively.[17] The wide income gap in the Arab region means that the distribution of the gains and losses from integration would be uneven across countries, thereby increasing opposition to integration. At one end, poor countries fear being marginalized. At the other, rich Arab countries, primarily oil-producing countries, are not motivated to share their wealth with poor countries without assured returns.[18]

Geographic Proximity

Arab countries are geographically close, with most having common borders. Yet high tariff barriers, lack of adequate infrastructure, and different means of transportation all increase the cost of trade between countries and erode the comparative advantage of proximity. In the cases of the EU and NAFTA, however, proximity—coupled with nonexistent tariffs and an intensive and diverse infrastructure network—played an important role in activating intraregional trade.

Openness to Trade

Arab economies are highly protected, both in absolute terms and in comparison with those of other developing countries. Although most of them have stepped up their liberalization efforts since the mid 1980s through unilateral, multilateral, and regional trade agreements, the average tariff for the region remains much higher than that of other regions (figure 2-3). Also, nontariff barriers are extensive in many countries in the region.[19] The high level of protection, a legacy of the import-substitution strategy pursued following independence in most Arab states, has had important implications. It makes integration undesirable because it means the loss of

17. Shafik (1994).
18. Alonso-Gamo and others (1997).
19. Zarrouk (1998).

Figure 2-3. Selected Indicators for Arab Countries and Other Regions, Average 1995–99

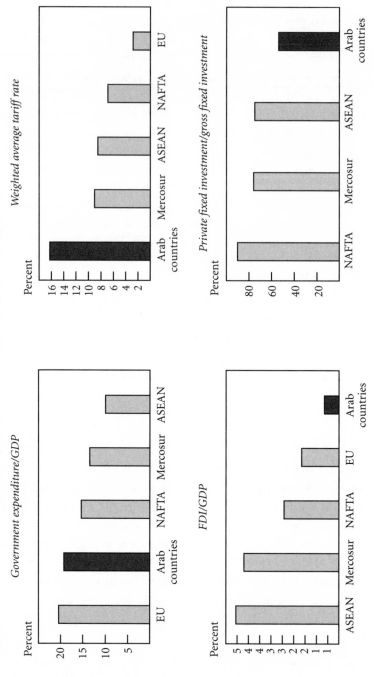

Government expenditure/GDP

Weighted average tariff rate

FDI/GDP

Private fixed investment/gross fixed investment

Source: United Nations, Comtrade database.

tariff revenues, which came to be a main source of revenue.[20] Industries, which survived behind high walls of protection, are likely to resist integration for fear of competition. Furthermore, high levels of protection reduce firms' incentives to trade, since their profits often are higher in sheltered markets. Finally, exports receive low priority, even when foreign exchange is a scarce commodity.[21]

In contrast, for both the EU and NAFTA openness to trade has preceded regionalism. The low level of tariffs meant that trade diversion was minimal under regional agreements. In the EU, tariffs already had been eliminated under the common market agreement in the 1950s and 1960s. Before NAFTA, average tariffs on Mexican goods entering the United States were about 4 percent and about 10 percent for U.S. goods entering Mexico. In addition, considerable effort was exerted to eliminate quotas in both cases.[22]

Private Sector Participation in Economic Activity

Although review of successful regional blocs illustrates the importance of the private sector in the integration process, the role of the private sector in the Arab world remains limited and governments continue to dominate economic activity. The large size of government, measured by government expenditures as a percentage of GDP, has had the effect of crowding out the private sector (figure 2-3). Furthermore, the shortcomings of the institutions and legal framework for investment have led to a lack of transparency, high transaction costs, and an uncompetitive business sector. Beyond its limited size and poor competitiveness, the private sector may also have found integration within the region unappealing. For example, in most countries the business environment remains less hospitable than elsewhere. Local markets also are more attractive than those in neighboring countries, largely because of protection.[23]

---

20. Because tariffs in most Arab countries account for a sizeable share of government revenue, nearly 20 percent on average for the period 1995–97, governments were reluctant to give up this stable source of financial resources.

21. Hoekman (1998).

22. Shafik (1994).

23. Furthermore, several studies have shown that many factors were working to reinforce the slow progress of Arab integration. One was the debt crisis that hit a number of Arab countries during the 1980s as a result of falling oil prices. It hit Egypt and Jordan particularly badly because they relied heavily on Arab aid and migrant remittances (Owen 1999).

In contrast to the absence of a business interest in Arab economic integration, private enterprises played an important role in the process of integration in Europe and America.[24] In the EU, private firms supported the Treaty of Rome. A group of Europe's largest firms, arguing that a fragmented Europe deprived them of the economies of scale they needed to be competitive, helped in revitalizing the integration process in Europe, which led to the signing of the Single European Act in 1986.

Similarly, in the case of NAFTA, governments brought business into the negotiating process in a well-designed and clear way. The governments decided that all tariffs would be removed and all quotas abolished, and private industries prepared position papers as part of the negotiations concerning the timing and order of actions. Big business organizations in NAFTA—including the National Association of Manufacturers, the National Retail Federation, the Business Roundtable, and the U.S. Council for International Business—expressed support for deeper integration by asking to have the agreement extended to encompass various guarantees, for example, regarding the availability of foreign exchange, expropriation, and dispute settlement.[25]

From the preceding discussion, it is clear that Arab countries did not have sufficient economic incentives to seek regional integration. The low degree of openness to trade, low level of complementarity, and limited role of the private sector were the main disincentives to integrate. But economics is not the only driving force for integration; politics is just as important.

Political Incentives

According to the political science literature on economic integration, three main conditions are necessary for integration to occur.[26] First, political leaders must be willing to integrate. Second, they should be able to establish an effective regional institutional framework to resolve any problems that may accompany integration. Third, they must accept voluntarily that one or more members of the group will act as regional leader.

24. Mattli (2000).
25. Lawrence (1997).
26. Haas (1968); Moravcisk (1991).

—*Political willingness to integrate.* The willingness of political leaders to integrate requires that the potential benefits, in terms of retaining political power or improving election chances, exceed the expected costs of integration. In other words, political leaders are likely to encourage integration if it enhances their legitimacy without too much loss of sovereignty.

—*Regional institutional framework.* Leaders must be able to establish supranational regional rules, policies, and organizations to formulate and monitor policies as well as resolve disputes. The institutions' main mandate would be to pursue integration, mobilize the support of different countries, and ensure enforcement of regional rules.

—*Voluntary acceptance of regional leadership.* Regional integration schemes may go beyond removing border barriers (shallow integration) to adopt common regulations and policies (deep integration), such as common rules of origin, commercial policies, and investment codes. This often gives rise to coordination problems, especially when states have conflicting interests and views about the appropriate course of action. The best solution to the problem is to agree on the leadership of one state or more whose support is perceived to be important to ensuring that the agreement will stand. The leader or leaders can serve to coordinate rules, regulations, and policies and also help ease distributional tensions—for example, through the use of compensatory measures.

Available evidence supports this theoretical framework. Countries that have integrated successfully satisfied these three conditions; it therefore seems plausible to attribute the slow progress of Arab integration to the lack of all three conditions, which is explored below.

Political Will

The decision to integrate implies the sacrifice of a certain degree of political autonomy. Therefore, for integration to be politically desirable, its potential benefits to leaders and their constituencies in terms of retaining political power or increasing the chances of reelection must outweigh its expected costs. In the Arab region, however, it seems that the benefits of integration are likely to be less than the costs. The economic gains associated with integration are likely to be relatively small, which may explain in part why leaders have not been eager to integrate. In contrast, EU and NAFTA leaders considered the potential economic gains to be significant.

The European countries adopted the Single European Act in response to slow European economic growth in the early 1980s; similarly, Canada and Mexico turned to the United States when their economies were in trouble.[27] More important, as Escribano points out, because most Arab leaders are not freely elected, they do not necessarily see welfare gains from integration, if any, to be the main way to stay in power.[28]

As for expected costs, the fear of losing sovereignty is considered the main obstacle to integration. According to Hudson and Sayigh, the ruling elites in the Arab world, with their vested interest in maintaining their own influence within their individual states, were less than supportive of integration projects.[29] Often they held the conviction that to be effective, economic integration must be accompanied sooner or later by political integration. For the elite, that would mean losing their privileged class position.[30]

Another important obstacle is that integration often leads, in the short and the medium terms, to some transitional costs that can result in social pressures that are too high from a political point of view. Tariff cuts, widening external imbalances, downsizing of import-substitution industries, and rising unemployment are some examples of the costs of adjustment. Although in the long run benefits may outweigh short-run costs, the long run may prove longer than politicians are willing to admit. That is true of the experiences of all regional entities, but it may be more pronounced in the Arab region because of the significant need for adjustment to allow countries to benefit from integration. The absence of mechanisms to compensate those who lose out through integration exacerbates the problem for political leaders.

Examples of these costs are indicated in table 2-4, which shows, by proxy, the significant weight of the groups that are most likely to oppose integration in the Arab world and that seem to have the power to block it. They include import-substituting industrialists (weight measured by manufactured exports as a share of total exports as a proxy), bureaucrats responsible for fiscal sustainability (weight measured by import duties as a percent-

27. Mattli (2000).
28. Escribano (2000).
29. Hudson (1999); Sayigh (1999).
30. Sirageldin (1998) and Escribano (2000) have cited other political reasons that discourage Arab governments from seeking integration, such as internal unrest, fragmentation, and lack of mutual trust.

Table 2-4. *Selected Indicators for the Arab Region and Other Regions*

Percent

Indicator	Region	Average (1995–99)
Manufacturing exports/total exports	Arab countries	24
	EU	82
	NAFTA	75
	Mersosur	31
	ASEAN	66
Import duties/tax revenue	Arab countries	30
	EU	n.a.
	NAFTA	2
	Mercosur	6
	ASEAN	15
Unemployment/total labor force	Arab countries	22
	EU	n.a.
	NAFTA	6
	Mercosur	8
	ASEAN	4

Source: World Bank, *World Development Indicators,* 2001 (CD-ROM).

age of tax revenues as a proxy), and employees in the government and public sector (weight measured by the unemployment rate as a proxy).

Regional Commitment Institutions

Commitment institutions are the various organizations in a regional arrangement whose rules and policies are hierarchically superior to domestic
law and directly applicable to members. Their main responsibility is to
monitor compliance and enforce regional integration obligations. The
availability of such institutions in the Arab region is reviewed below.

REGIONAL MONITORING AND ENFORCING INSTITUTIONS. Although
there are many Arab regional organizations (for example, the Arab Economic Council, Economic and Social Council, Organization of Petroleum
Exporting Countries, Arab Labor Organization, Arab Institution for Investment Guarantees, and Arab Fund for Social and Economic Development),
the region lacks effective institutions to deal with formulating, implementing, and monitoring the rules, laws, and policies necessary for regional integration to take place. In contrast, member states in the EU established

supranational institutions—such as the Commission of the European Communities and the European Council (the executive authority of the EU), the European Parliament (the legislative authority), and the European Court of Justice (the judicial authority)—which have played a major role in the development and success of the EU.[31]

It seems that in the Arab region the problem is the existence of too many organizations with insignificant roles and capacity and hence insignificant results. Because economic and political incentives to integrate were largely absent in the first place, that is not the real barrier to integration, but the lack of an effective institutional framework may inhibit any attempts to speed up the integration process in the future.

Of course, the Arab countries formed the Arab League many years ago; however, the league's efforts to foster economic integration generally have not been very effective.[32] The league is not a supranational organization like the European Commission. It lacks the legal and political authority to override the sovereignty of its member states; in fact, the preamble of the league's charter ensures their sovereignty and independence. Furthermore, it is a relatively small organization, encompassing only about 1,000 employees; the European Union, in contrast, has 20,000 employees in Brussels alone. In addition, the league does not have the collective policymaking institutions and related mechanisms required for regional conflict resolution.

COMPENSATION MECHANISMS. Neither the 1981 Agreement for Facilitation and Promotion of Intra-Arab Trade nor the 1997 GAFTA agreement provides effective mechanisms to compensate those who would lose as a result of integration, a fact that led a number of countries to refrain from liberalizing their trade. Evidence from other regional blocs supports this finding. The Latin American Free Trade Area Association and the Andean Pact eventually collapsed due to disagreements regarding how costs and benefits of the arrangements were being shared among members. The nonexistence of mechanisms to deal with the distribution of gains within each country also have hindered efforts for Arab regional integration.

In the EU, the use of instruments to compensate those who lose from integration has been an important element of its success. Two types of instruments were employed, the first to compensate losers within countries

31. Hoekman and Messerlin, chapter 6 in this volume.
32. Hudson (1999).

and the second to compensate losing countries or regions.[33] An example of the former is the common agricultural policy (CAP), created to compensate the agricultural sector. Germany, Britain, and the Netherlands were net contributors to CAP, while France, Italy, and Ireland were the main beneficiaries. Examples of the latter include the European Investment Bank (EIB) and the European Social Fund (ESF), which were intended to assist less developed regions as well as areas affected by industrial decline and high unemployment. The major beneficiaries were Portugal, Spain, Greece, and Ireland.

With NAFTA, there were no financial compensation schemes for Mexico. Instead, Mexico was granted more time to adjust through a more gradual phasing of trade liberalization. For example, while the United States was supposed to eliminate tariffs on many products immediately, Mexico was given a period of up to five years to eliminate tariffs on some products.

Regional Leadership

According to Hudson, the Arab region lacks uncontested regional leadership.[34] This lack of leadership has also crippled the Latin America Free Trade Area, ASEAN, and the Andean Pact. Egypt in part played such a role for the Arab region in the 1950s and 1960s; however, this role declined significantly following Egypt's signing of the peace treaty with Israel in 1978.

Since then, several other Arab countries—including Iraq, Syria, and Saudi Arabia—have seemed to believe that they qualify to play a leading role. Iraq had begun to emerge as a potential core state, but after its defeat in the Gulf war the possibility of assuming the role of regional leader was lost. Syria is a leading power in the western Fertile Crescent, but its relatively low level of development prevents it from acting as a regional leader. Saudi Arabia has a special position among the Gulf states but not in the region as a whole.

In contrast, the existence of one or two regional leaders among member states was one of the key reasons behind the success of the EU, whose leaders were Germany and France, and NAFTA, whose leader was the United States.[35] It was less costly politically and economically to adapt to the leaders'

33. Shafik (1994).
34. Hudson (1999).
35. Mattli (2000).

policies. For example, switching to German safety standards was less costly to the EU than switching to Dutch standards. Also, Germany has been the key initiator of policy for the European monetary system. That and the calling for an intergovernmental conference on a political union paralleling the proposed European Monetary Union (EMU) were considered the first acts of German leadership in the history of the EU. The existence of a regional leader also helped ease distributional tensions and thus smoothed the path of integration. Germany is by far the largest net contributor to the European Development Fund (EDF) and the European Social Fund.

Looking Forward

Although regional integration has gained momentum all over the world, Arab regional integration remains limited and compares unfavorably with that in other regional blocs, raising concerns about the Arab region's future. It also has triggered a search for an explanation of the region's unsatisfactory record on economic integration.

The Arab region remains the least integrated of all, whether in terms of trade or factor movements, and the lack of both economic and political incentives is responsible for the slow progress to date. More specifically, six economic and political factors can be seen as the major reasons behind the limited tangible results in the past: the low degree of complementarity among Arab countries; low level of openness to trade; weakness in the role of the private sector; unwillingness of political leaders to integrate; shortage of commitment institutions, in particular the absence of mechanisms to compensate those who lose from integration; and finally, the lack of consensus on choosing a regional leader or leaders.

The future, however, seems more promising. This view is based on the more favorable internal and external economic circumstances currently prevailing and on some positive political changes.

—*The economic front.* The last decade witnessed considerable economic reform in several countries, including Egypt, Jordan, Morocco, Tunisia, and Lebanon. Reforms involved significant progress toward trade liberalization through unilateral, multilateral, and regional efforts. At present, eleven Arab countries are full members of the WTO, of which six have signed association agreements with the EU. A key benefit of both arrangements is their potential role as a commitment device, harmonizing the countries' domestic laws and standards with international norms. More specifically, the establishment of the association agreements between the EU and some Arab countries is expected to increase motivation for regional integration among Arab countries as this will enable them to benefit fully from the agreements.

The reforms also created new roles for both the government and the private sector that probably will have many positive implications. For example, governments will be relieved from engaging in production-related activities. That will enable them to concentrate more on getting the fundamentals right—that is, improving the business environment and providing the necessary hard and soft infrastructure, which are highlighted in many studies as preconditions for fostering regional integration. Moreover, the increasing participation of the private sector in economic activities probably will improve productivity and increase nontraditional exports. Finally, the possibility of private involvement in regional infrastructure projects could serve to promote the creation of regional arrangements, given that the current lack of infrastructure is considered one of the most critical impediments to regional cooperation. Equally important, the 1997 GAFTA agreement involves, for the first time, commitments by Arab countries to reduce tariff rates by a yearly average of 10 percent over a period of ten years. Although each member country is allowed to draw up a list of agricultural and manufactured products to be protected during a transition period, that protection is to disappear by 2008. GAFTA also calls for the elimination of nontariff barriers and the exchange of trade information. In addition, it establishes guidelines for settling disputes, defining rules of origin, and extending favorable treatment to the least developed countries.[36]

—*The political front.* There is a growing understanding in some Arab political circles that it is difficult for any country to isolate itself from the current wave of globalization and that the regional approach outweighs the individual country approach to participation in the world market. This shift is evident in different initiatives to liberalize multilaterally and regionally. Different groups (for example, intellectuals and political parties) in many Arab countries have realized that regionalism carries political weight—that it can increase the region's collective bargaining power. It seems that the higher educational level of the younger generation in several countries has positively influenced public opinion and general attitudes.

36. Zarrouk (1998).

Furthermore, recent changes in some Arab countries have generated great expectations for accelerating liberal political reforms. In Morocco, a new government has been democratically elected in conjunction with the accession of Mohamed VI to the throne; the prime minister in the new cabinet, Abdel Rahman El Youssefi, was a prominent member of the opposition in Morocco. In Jordan and Syria, more liberal leadership has come to power with King Abdullah and President Bashar, respectively. In Egypt, the 2000 election of the People's Assembly has been considered a stepping stone to ward a more democratic regime. In addition, the implementation of economic reform programs in some countries—such as Egypt, Morocco, Tunisia, Jordan, and Lebanon—has weakened the relative importance of interest groups opposing economic reform. All of these changes have created a political environment that is more supportive of regional integration.

Although the current economic and political situations increase the likelihood of successful Arab integration in the future, much remains to be done to realize its potential. Unless existing barriers and new challenges are seriously addressed, Arab integration will remain a hope rather than a reality. The most important challenges facing the future of Arab integration include the implementation of further domestic economic reforms and the development of a strong political will to integrate.

Indeed, the policy implication of the analysis is that Arab countries should work on two tracks at once: the domestic and the regional. Domestically, efforts should be devoted to liberalization, deregulation, and acceleration of structural reforms, particularly those affecting private investment. Undertaking such reforms not only will help create economic incentives to integrate but also help to motivate leaders. Economic reforms would result in larger potential benefits from integration, which most probably would have a positive influence on leaders. While domestic reforms are key to greater Arab economic interaction, several regional measures also are crucial: establishing mechanisms for compensating the losers in integration; strengthening the regional institutional framework; and moving toward greater depth in the GAFTA agreement. Finally, it is essential to note that without political support, Arab integration will stay in the virtual domain.

In a nutshell, regionalism has become one of the rules governing the global economic and political game. Arab countries therefore need to make the choice to integrate. The current economic and political circumstances offer greater potential for success in the future; however, success will require extensive effort. Integration is not an isolated event; it is a long process that demands immediate and continuous action.

References

Al-Atrash, H., and Tarik Yousef. 2000. "Intra-Arab Trade: Is It Too Little?" IMF Working Paper 00/10. Washington: International Monetary Fund (January).

Al-Monzery, Soliman. 1995. "Lost Opportunities in Economic Integration and the Arab Development Path." Cairo (in Arabic).

Alonso-Gamo, Patricia, Annalisa Fedelino, and Sebastian Paris Horvitz. 1997. "Globalization and Growth Prospects in Arab Countries." IMF Working Paper 125. Washington: International Monetary Fund.

Arab League. Various years. *The Arab Economic Consolidated Report.* Cairo.

De Melo, Jaime, and Arvind Panagariya. 1993. "Introduction." In *New Dimensions in Regional Integration*, edited by Jaime De Melo and Arvind Panagariya, 3–20. Cambridge University Press.

Devlin, Julia, and John Page. 2001. "Testing the Waters: Arab Integration, Competitiveness, and the Euro-Med Agreements." In *Towards Arab and Euro-Med Regional Integration*, edited by Sebastian Dessus, Julia Devlin, and Raed Safadi. Paris: Organization for Economic Cooperation and Development.

El Erian, Mohamed, and Stanley Fischer. 1996. "Is MENA a Region? The Scope for Regional Integration." IMF Working Paper 30. Washington: International Monetary Fund.

El Naggar, Said. 1997. "Foreign and Intra-trade Policies of the Arab Countries: The Basic Issues." In *Foreign and Intra-Trade Policies of the Arab Countries*, edited by Said El-Naggar. Washington: International Monetary Fund.

Escribano, Gonzalo. 2000. "Euro-Mediterranean versus Arab Integration: Are They Compatible?" Paper presented at the International Conference on Arab Development Challenges of the New Millennium. Rabat, Morocco, June 26–28.

Galal, Ahmed, and Bernard Hoekman. 1997. "Egypt and the Partnership Agreement with the EU: The Road to Maximum Benefits." In *Regional Partners in Global Markets: Limits and Possibilities of the Euro-Med Agreements*, edited by Ahmed Galal and Bernard Hoekman, 282–306. London: Center for Economic Policy Research and the Egyptian Center for Economic Studies.

Haas, Ernst. 1968. *The Uniting of Europe.* Stanford University Press.

Havrylyshyn, Oleh, and Peter Kunzel. 2000. "Intra-Industry Trade of Arab Countries: An Indicator of Potential Competitiveness." In *Catching Up with the Competition: Trade Opportunities and Challenges for Arab Countries*, edited by Bernard Hoekman and J. Zarrouk. University of Michigan Press.

Hoekman, Bernard. 1998. "The World Trade Organization, the European Union, and the Arab World." In *Prospects for MENA Economies*, edited by Nemaat Shafik. London: Macmillan.

Hoekman, Bernard, and others. 1998. "Economic Incentives and Effects." In *Building Bridges: An Egypt-U.S. Free Trade Agreement*, edited by Ahmed Galal and Robert Z. Lawrence, 79–110. Brookings.

Hudson, Michael. 1999. "Introduction: Arab Integration: An Overview." In *The Middle East Dilemma*, edited by Michael Hudson. Center for Contemporary Arab Studies, Georgetown University.

Konan, Denise, and Keith Maskus. 1997. "A Computable General Equilibrium Analysis of Egyptian Trade Liberalization Scenarios." In *Regional Partners in Global Markets: Limits and Possibilities of the Euro-Med Agreements*, edited by Ahmed Galal and Bernard Hoekman, 156–177. London: Center for Economic Policy Research and the Egyptian Center for Economic Studies.

Lawrence, Robert. 1997. "Preferential Trading Arrangements: The Traditional and the New." In *Regional Partners in Global Markets: Limits and Possibilities of the Euro-Med Agreements*, edited by Ahmed Galal and Bernard Hoekman, 13–34. London: Center for Economic Policy Research and the Egyptian Center for Economic Studies.

Mattli, Walter. 2000. "A Comparative Analysis for Regional Integration: What Lessons for the Arab Region?" In *Arab Development: Challenges of the New Millennium*, edited by Laabas Belkacem. Burlington, Vt.: Ashgate.

Moravcisk, Andrew. 1991. "Negotiating the Single European Act." *International Organization* 5: 19–56.

Owen, Roger. 1999. "Inter-Arab Economic Relations during the Twentieth Century: World Market vs. Regional Market." In *The Middle East Dilemma*, edited by Michael Hudson. Center for Contemporary Arab Studies, Georgetown University.

Said, Edward. "Arab Powerlessness." *Al-Ahram Weekly*, April 25, 1996. Cairo.

Sayigh, Yusif. 1999. "Arab Economic Integration: The Poor Harvest of the 1980s." In *The Middle East Dilemma*, edited by Michael Hudson. Center for Contemporary Arab Studies, Georgetown University.

Shafik, Nemaat. 1994. "Learning from Doers: Lessons on Regional Integration for the Middle East." Paper prepared for the conference "Economic Cooperation in the Middle East: Prospects and Challenges." Cairo University, May 14–16.

Sirageldin, Ismail. 1998. "Globalization, Regionalism, and Recent Trade Agreements: Impact on Arab Economies." Working Paper 98/7. Cairo: Economic Research Forum for the Arab Countries, Iran, and Turkey.

Viner, Jacob. 1950. *The Customs Union Issue*. New York: Carnegie Endowment for International Peace.

Yeats, Alexander, and Francis Ng. 2000. "Beyond the Year 2000: Implications of the Middle East's Recent Trade Performance." In *Catching Up with the Competition:*

Trade Opportunities and Challenges for Arab Countries, edited by Bernard Hoekman and Jamel Zarrouk, 9–44. University of Michigan Press.

Zarrouk, Jamel. 1992. "Intra-Trade: Determinants and Prospects for Expansion." In *Foreign and Intra-Trade Policies of the Arab Countries,* edited by Said El-Naggar. Washington: International Monetary Fund.

———. 1998. "Arab Free Trade Area: Potentialities and Effects." Paper prepared for the Mediterranean Development Forum, Morocco.

3

Egypt's Export Puzzle

AHMED GALAL
SAMIHA FAWZY

The Egyptian government has voiced its commitment to export pro-motion. Senior government officials have stated that exporting is a "matter of life and death" for the Egyptian economy, and over the last ten years they have backed that statement by sustained efforts to reduce the bias against exports through such measures as trade liberalization; adoption of duty drawback, tax rebate, and temporary admission schemes; and simplification of customs procedures. Yet the export record does not reflect their commitment to reform. Exports have not grown sufficiently to generate the foreign exchange needed to boost economic development. Clearly something is not working—either reform measures are not well designed, the measures taken are insufficient, or a mix of both.

This chapter does not seek to identify the variables that impair Egyptian exports. Several studies have identified those variables, which include lack of exchange rate competitiveness, high levels of protection, excessive costs of transport and communication, and large transaction costs in dealing with

This chapter was first published in the Policy Viewpoint series of the Egyptian Center for Economic Studies in 2002. The authors would like to thank Amal Refaat, Nada Masoud, and Noha Sherif for valuable research assistance.

customs and tax administrations. Rather, it attempts to estimate the extent and origin of the disincentives to export, with a view to proposing a set of actions to deal with the most important disincentives. The analysis is guided by the simple notion that producers favor selling in domestic markets because prices and cost structures make it more attractive to sell at home than abroad. Any measures to change their behavior will have to improve their bottom line. Measures that have only a marginal affect on profitability are not likely to make a noticeable difference.

The chapter first reviews the export performance record over the 1990s. Next, an attempt is made to explain the record by comparing the rates of return of two hypothetical producers: one is an exporter and the other sells exclusively in domestic markets. The analysis compares the effects of Egypt's export incentive structure on profitability with the effects of the structures of other developing countries. On the basis of the above, the chapter simulates the impact of different variables on the profitability of Egyptian exporters in an attempt to identify reform priorities.

Export Performance

The export figures for the 1990s bring both good and bad news. The good news is that exports increased in absolute terms, up from US$4.2 billion in 1990–91 to US$6.3 billion in 1999–2000. The composition and geographical destination of exports also have become more diversified. In terms of composition, the share of manufactured exports to total exports increased from 27 percent in 1990–91 to 45 percent in 1999–2000, while the importance of traditional resource-based exports—such as crude oil and agriculture and mining products—declined from 40 percent in 1990–91 to 19 percent in 1997–98. With respect to geographical distribution, the share of EU countries to total exports decreased from 35 percent in 1990–91 to 26 percent in 1999–2000, while the share of Middle Eastern and North African countries and the United States increased from 16 and 8 percent to 45 and 16 percent, respectively.[1]

The bad news is that the growth rates of Egyptian exports were very small relative to the growth in GDP. Consequently, the share of merchandise exports to GDP decreased sharply, from 14 percent in 1990–91 to around

1. Egyptian Ministry of Economy and Foreign Trade (2000).

Figure 3-1. *Exports as a Percent of GDP in Egypt, 1990–91 to 1999–2000*

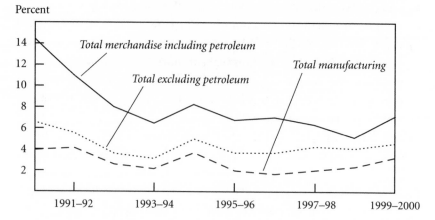

Source: Egyptian Ministry of Economy and Foreign Trade (2000).

7 percent in 1999–2000 (figure 3-1). When oil exports are excluded, the figure goes down to 4.7 percent. The share of manufactured exports to GDP also fell from 4 percent in 1990–91 to 3.3 percent in 1999–2000. Moreover, the basket of Egyptian exports did not reflect changes in world demand. A 2000 World Bank study points out that 32 percent of Egypt's exports were growing, while world consumption was declining; and, nearly 17 percent of Egyptian exports were declining, while world consumption of these commodities was increasing.[2]

A comparison of the performance of Egyptian exports with those of other countries supports the conclusion that Egypt could do better. The figures in table 3-1 indicate that while per capita export in Egypt ($63) does exceed that of South Asia ($40), it is much less than per capita export elsewhere in the world, including sub-Saharan Africa ($122). A similar point can be made with respect to the share of merchandise exports to GDP, the share of manufactured exports to total exports, and the share of high-tech exports to manufactured exports. Egyptian exports have lost their competitive position in the world market as their share in world exports declined from 0.11 percent in 1990 to 0.09 percent in 1999.[3]

2. World Bank (2000).
3. International Monetary Fund, *International Financial Statistics,* 2000.

Table 3-1. *Export Performance Indicators, 1996–99*

Percent, unless otherwise indicated

Region	Average merchandise exports to GDP, 1996–99	Average manufacturing exports to total merchandise exports, 1996–99	Average high-tech exports to manufacturing exports, 1998–99	Per capita exports, 1996–99 (US$)
East Asia and Pacific	28.5	77.5	29.5	266.7
Europe and Central Asia	24.1	55.3	10.0	531.4
Latin America and Caribbean	13.9	47.8	14.0	562.7
Middle East and North Africa	23.9	19.0	1.5	466.4
South Asia	9.8	77.3	4.0	40.5
Sub-Saharan Africa	23.6	39.0	9.0	122.2
Egypt	4.9	39.0	0.0	63.3

Source: World Bank, *World Development Indicators,* 2001.

Why Are Egyptian Producers Not Exporting? A Simple Answer

Some analysts attribute the disappointing track record of Egyptian exports to the inability of local firms to compete because of outdated technology, management techniques, and marketing strategies. They conclude that even if exporters were offered sufficient price incentives, they would not respond (the low elasticity of supply argument). The logical conclusion on the basis of that argument is that firms have to become more competitive before attention is turned to reducing the anti-export bias.

But that view of the problem is partial at best. There is strong evidence that exports typically go up when governments reduce or eliminate anti-export bias.[4] Firms do adjust to changes in incentives, once favorable incentives are put in place and rents from producing for local markets diminish. The question for Egypt is whether the trade liberalization of the 1990s and the adoption of the export duty drawback, tax rebate, and temporary admission schemes have sufficiently reduced the anti-export bias.

4. For example, Edwards (1994).

The method followed to estimate this bias is simple. It calculates, on the basis of the current incentive structure, the rates of return on equity (ROE) and return on assets (ROA) of two identical producers, both of whom are engaged in manufacturing and operate inland. The first produces entirely for the overseas market; the second produces entirely for the domestic market. The two producers have the same output, cost structure, and balance sheet. They operate under the same parameters, including corporate tax rates, borrowing rates, and depreciation rates. They differ in two respects only. First, the exporter's revenues are generated in the international market at world prices. The exporter is assumed to obtain all intermediate inputs under the temporary admission scheme. Therefore, he or she does not pay any tariffs or sales taxes on imports but does incur the cost of a letter of guarantee at a rate of 1.2 percent of the value of these imports for a year (six months for the production cycle and six months for settlement), as well as the cost of the cash held in the bank to cover the letter of guarantee.[5]

In comparison, the producer for the local market is able to charge the international price, plus tariffs and surcharges on imports, subject to the price elasticity of local demand. (Results are simulated under three price elasticities of demand: –1, –0.9, and –1.1.) The producer is not exempted from tariffs or sales tax on imported intermediate inputs. The results of the simulation are presented in table 3-2.

In all three scenarios, the producer for the domestic market has a higher ROE and ROA than the producer for the overseas market. The difference is greatest when the price elasticity of demand is less than one, reaching an ROE of 60.1 percent for the producer for the home market compared with 19.0 percent for the exporter. This difference diminishes when the consumers are responsive to price hikes (elasticity is larger than one, specifically –1.1). But even then, the producer for the domestic market has an ROE of 24.9 percent compared with 19.0 percent for the exporter. These results indicate that the protection afforded to producers for the domestic market through tariffs offset by a substantial margin the partial compensation offered to exporters under the temporary admission scheme. The trade liberalization effort of the 1990s has yet to significantly reduce the bias against exports.

5. Banks require varying cash coverage, depending on the exporter's track record. We assume an average coverage requirement of 50 percent of tariffs and sales taxes and a 13 percent borrowing rate.

Table 3-2. *Rates of Return to Two Identical Producers*
Percent

	Exporter	Domestic market producer		
		Elasticity −1	Elasticity −1.1	Elasticity −0.9
Return on equity	19.0	43.3	24.9	60.1
Return on assets	4.8	10.4	6.0	14.5

Source: Authors' calculations.

These conclusions hold on average for all industries. Results will vary for specific industries depending, among other variables, on the relevant debt/equity structure, the share of imported intermediate inputs to total cost, the level of tariff and para-tariff rates on final products and imported inputs, and the specific demand elasticity. By way of illustration only, the exercise is carried out for the food processing and leather products sectors (table 3-3). Although the ROE results for these industries vary in magnitude from the average results for the economy, the main conclusion remains: it is more profitable for Egyptian producers to sell at home than to export.

Another Simple Answer

Another way of explaining the sluggish growth of exports in Egypt is to compare the impact on profitability of the incentive structures facing Egyptian exporters and their counterparts in developing countries. This approach has two main merits. It highlights the need for reforming national policies (for example, the exchange rate, tariffs and surcharges on intermediate inputs, tax rebate and temporary admission schemes, the cost of capital, and profit tax

Table 3-3. *Rates of Return on Equity to Two Identical Producers in Different Industries*
Percent

	Exporter	Domestic market producer		
		Elasticity −1	Elasticity −1.1	Elasticity −0.9
Food processing	19.0	34.0	20.5	47.6
Leather products	16.8	37.5	18.2	56.8

Source: Authors' calculations.

Table 3-4. *Parameters Affecting Exporters in Egypt and Other Developing Countries*
Percent

Parameters/variables	Egypt	Developing countries
Exchange rate (£E/US$)	3.85[a]	
Tariffs, surcharges, and sales taxes		
Tariff on intermediate inputs	21.0	12.5
Tariff on machinery and equipment	10.0	11.5
Surcharge on output	3.0	2.7
Surcharge on intermediate inputs	3.0	2.7
Sales tax on intermediate input	10.0	9.7
Sales tax on machinery and equipment	10.0	9.7
Interest rate (on short- and medium-term loans in local currency)	13.0	12.2
Profit taxes	34.0	26.3

Sources: All variables are from the European Commission website (http://mkaccdb.eu.int [November 13, 2002]), except for interest rates, which are taken from International Monetary Fund, *International Financial Statistics*, 2000.

a. The unofficial market rate is £E4.05 to the U.S. dollar.

rate) and national institutions (for example, customs administration and tax administration). In addition, it draws attention to the inefficiencies of domestically produced goods and services, especially of nontradable services such as financial, port, and local transport and communication services.

To find out whether the incentive structure in Egypt favors Egyptian exporters over their competitors, key variables for Egypt and twenty-seven developing countries are first examined (table 3-4).[6] On the basis of this information, it is clear that Egyptian tariffs, surcharges, and sales taxes on intermediate inputs and capital goods are higher than the average for this sample of countries. In addition, Egyptian exporters face higher interest rates on loans in local currency and higher profit tax rates. It also is probable that most Egyptian exporters face a modest overvaluation of the pound, if the unofficial market rate is taken as an indicator of equilibrium exchange rate.

6. The list of countries includes India, Bangladesh, and China in Asia; Morocco and Israel in the Middle East; Mexico, Brazil, and Argentina in Latin America; and Poland, Hungary, and Bulgaria in eastern Europe.

Table 3-5. *Return on Equity to Egyptian
and Developing Country Exporters*

Percent

Exporters from	With exemption[a]	Without exemption
Egypt	19.0	8.1
Developing countries	28.6	18.8

Source: Authors' calculations.

a. Exemption of tariffs and sales tax on imported inputs and capital.

Notably, this list does not include some of the cost items frequently cited by Egyptian exporters as excessive in comparison with those of other countries, such as customs and tax administration and the cost of port services, storage facilities, and local transport. These variables are omitted because of the lack of unbiased and consistent data for our sample of countries. Their inclusion would have further increased the less-than-favorable treatment received by Egyptian exporters.

But even with the set of variables identified in table 3-4, the results of the following simulation indicate that the incentive structure in Egypt does not support exporters compared with the structures of their competitors. In table 3-5, the results are presented for exporters from Egypt and other developing countries, with and without exemptions from tariffs and sales tax on imported inputs and capital. Where the Egyptian and other developing country exporters benefit from the exemption, the Egyptian exporter has an ROE of only 19.0 percent compared with 28.6 percent for the developing country exporter. When neither benefits from the exemption, the Egyptian exporter makes a modest 8.1 percent compared with 18.8 percent for the competitor. The situation is much worse for the Egyptian exporter when only the competitors receive the exemption. The single situation in which the Egyptian exporter essentially breaks even with the developing country exporter is when the Egyptian exporter benefits from the temporary admission scheme and the developing country exporter does not.

Reform Priorities

The analysis so far suggests that even if Egyptian exporters benefit from the temporary admission scheme, they prefer to sell at home because of the high

Table 3-6. *Effect of a 10 Percent Change in Policy Variables on Exporter's Base Return on Equity of 19 Percent*
Percent

Policy variable	New ROE	Percent change in ROE	Absolute change in ROE
Exchange rate	22.94	20.71	3.94
Tariff, output[a]	40.13	−7.32	−3.17
Profit tax	19.98	5.15	0.98
Tariff, input	19.69	3.65	0.69
Sales tax, input	19.36	1.91	0.36
Letter of guarantee	19.09	0.50	0.09
Sales tax, capital goods	19.04	0.20	0.04
Tariff, capital goods	19.04	0.20	0.04

Source: Authors' calculations.
a. Calculated for the import-substituting firm, starting from a return on equity of 43.3 percent.

protection afforded to import-substituting firms. It also suggests that Egyptian exporters, compared with those in other developing countries, endure additional costs in securing imported inputs and capital, pay higher profit tax, and possibly forgo some revenue due to overvaluation of the pound. For policymakers who are keen on tackling policy variables that would have the most positive effects on exporters, it is a question of where to start.

One way of answering that question is to calculate the impact on profitability of changing the policy variables by the same percentage—say, 10 percent. The results are reported in table 3-6. Their interpretation is straightforward. A 10 percent devaluation of the pound brings about the greatest improvement in the bottom line for Egyptian exporters, followed by a 10 percent reduction in tariffs on imports of final goods, then by a 10 percent reduction in the profit tax rate. In contrast, a similar reduction of tariffs and sales tax on imported inputs and capital or a reduction in the time of holding the letter of guarantee in the temporary admission scheme brings only modest improvements.

These findings indicate that three areas most deserve government attention: the exchange rate, import tariffs on finished products, and the profit tax. Note that a reduction in the tariff rates on imports of finished products does not affect the exporter directly. It does, however, reduce the profitability of import-substituting firms, thereby making it more attractive for them to export. Furthermore, all other reforms would affect exporting and import-substituting firms alike, with the effect of enhancing their competitiveness in world markets.

Concluding Remarks

Increasing exports has been on top of the Egyptian government's agenda for years. Substantial effort also has been made to reduce the anti-export bias and increase the competitiveness of Egyptian firms through a host of policy and institutional reforms. The present analysis suggests, however, that reforms to date have not changed the incentive structure sufficiently to make it attractive for Egyptian firms to export. To reverse this trend, bold reforms are needed to accomplish the following:

—Change the incentive structure through further liberalizing the trade regime and maintaining a competitive real exchange rate. Pursuing trade liberalization through bilateral agreements is not necessarily the best way forward. Similarly, partial measures to reduce the bias against exports—for example, by refining the tax rebate or through temporary admission schemes—are inadequate and may not bring about tangible results.

—Improve the competitiveness of all Egyptian producers, exporters and others, through the reduction of the corporate tax rate, deregulation, corporatization, and in some cases privatization of key services (for example, port and financial services), as well as reform of relevant institutions (for example, customs and tax administrations).

These reforms are complex and implementing them requires dedicated effort, but they are the surest way to boost exports. Experience in Egypt and elsewhere shows that piecemeal reforms, while useful, do not bring about tangible results. Postponing reforms until firms modernize simply translates into a long waiting period. Firms respond only to competitive pressure.

References

Edwards, Sebastian. 1994. *Trade and Industrial Policy Reform in Latin America.* Working Paper 4772. Cambridge, Mass.: National Bureau of Economic Research.

Egyptian Ministry of Economy and Foreign Trade. 2000. *Quarterly Economic Digest* (October–December).

World Bank. 2000. *Arab Republic of Egypt: Plan of Actions for Export Promotion.* Washington.

4

A Survey of Barriers to Trade and Investment in Arab Countries

JAMEL ZARROUK

Given the general weakness in data on nontariff barriers to trade and investment in the Arab countries—and in particular data on the prevalence and magnitude of barriers to intra-Arab trade and investment—surveys can provide valuable information on the additional costs associated with restrictive policies. This chapter reports the results of a survey that was undertaken in 2000 to improve understanding of the trading constraints that hinder the development of private businesses in the Arab countries. The purpose of the survey was threefold: first, to generate information on trading costs and trade policies that impose burdens on intraregional trade and investment; second, to shed further light on the operations of the intraregional trade agreements prevailing among many of the countries in

The views expressed in this chapter are those of the author and should not be attributed to the Arab Monetary Fund. The survey on which this chapter is based was undertaken by a team of professionals who visited companies in eight Arab countries to conduct interviews and monitor the completion of a detailed questionnaire. The survey was funded by the Council on Foreign Relations, New York, as part of a study on trade options for the Middle East and North Africa. The results of the survey were published in Hoekman and Messerlin (2002).

the region; and third, to identify the most important factors in intraregional investment decisions as well as the constraints perceived by Arab investors when they decide to invest in neighboring countries.

Costs associated with international trade include transaction costs resulting from inefficiencies in customs clearance procedures, land transport regulations, and requirements that prevent competition from foreign suppliers or raise the cost of services provided by local firms. Transaction costs also are associated with the red tape generated in the administration of complex documentary requirements such as rules of origin. These types of trading costs often are alleged to have a major negative effect on trade and investment, but information on their incidence is patchy at best. The absence of good information on the relative importance of different types of restrictive policies impedes the ability of policymakers to assign priority to needed reforms. The absence of data also makes it more difficult for researchers to determine the costs of policies that restrict trade and investment, both in terms of static resource misallocation and lower growth performance.

The survey was conducted in July–December 2000. A private enterprise questionnaire was designed and completed in Egypt, Gaza and the West Bank, Jordan, Lebanon, Saudi Arabia, Syria, Tunisia, and the United Arab Emirates (UAE).[1] The questionnaire involved some thirty to forty-five respondents in each country and was completed by companies randomly selected from a database of exporters and importers maintained by the Arab Trade Financing Program of the Arab Monetary Fund. In addition, interviews were conducted with key company managers.

The questionnaire focuses on transaction costs associated with cross-border trade in the region as well as the business environment in general. The questions are grouped into four main categories. The first set of questions deals with customs procedures, restrictions on overland transport and transit, and competition policy (for example, business licensing, exclusive distribution systems and restraints on parallel imports, and nationality requirements) as well as "informal" constraints (for example, corruption and political barriers). The second set is designed to examine the effectiveness of agreements that Arab governments signed to promote intraregional trade and investment. The third set addresses the relative intensity of the

---

1. A copy of the questionnaire may be obtained upon request from the author at jamel_zarrouk@yahoo.com.

barriers that are perceived to prevail on a bilateral country pair basis. The fourth set surveys the business environment that prevails when companies in the region decide to invest in neighboring countries.

The methodology is descriptive; it involves ranking the regulatory and administrative constraints that create additional burdens on intra-Arab trade and investment. Companies were asked to quantify where possible the impact of administrative costs (in terms of numbers of working hours and days as well as in monetary terms) and to provide information on the size of "informal" payments to customs, tax, and other officials. They also were asked to rank both the major factors affecting foreign investment decisions and the various constraints they confront in engaging in intra-Arab direct investment.

Survey Results

The questionnaire was completed by a total of 230 companies from the eight Arab countries selected. The profiles of the surveyed countries and companies, which are representative of the manufacturing and service sectors in each country, are presented in tables 4-1 and 4-2. The compiled results are reported in four main sections: traders'estimates of trading costs in the region, including barriers to trade in services; estimates of relative intensity of intraregional trade barriers on a bilateral country pair basis; assessment of the benefits or failures of regional trade agreements; and perception of the business environment for intraregional direct investment.

Trading Costs and Barriers to Trade in Services

The surveyed companies estimated average costs of trading in the region (excluding customs duties and domestic taxes on imports) to be about 10.6 percent of the value of trade (table 4-3). A breakdown of this overall estimate by type of trading activity reveals that the reported values are close in magnitude, suggesting that there is no significant difference in importers' and exporters' estimates of the approximate costs of trading in the region.

The compiled results rank the major sources of trading costs in descending order as follows: customs clearance; public sector corruption; mandatory product standards and certification of conformity; transshipment regulations; and entry visa restrictions for business visits. When companies were asked to rank the severity of a set of costly constraints including customs

Table 4-1. *Profile of Countries Sampled*

	Companies interviewed		
Country	Number	Percent of total	Cumulative percent
Egypt	41	17.8	17.8
Gaza–West Bank	20	8.7	26.5
Jordan	44	19.1	45.7
Lebanon	44	19.1	64.8
Saudi Arabia	7	3.0	67.8
Syria	14	6.1	73.9
Tunisia	30	13.0	87.0
UAE	30	13.0	100
Total	230	100	

Source: All tables in this chapter are based on the author's survey, as described in the text.

Table 4-2. *Profile of Companies Sampled, by Economic Activity*

	Companies interviewed		
Economic activity	Number	Percent of total	Cumulative percent
Manufacturing			
Textiles and garments	34	14.8	14.8
Furniture, paper products, leather, handicrafts	20	8.7	23.5
Agroprocessing, food, beverages	30	13.0	36.5
Chemicals, plastics, pharmaceuticals	28	12.2	48.7
Stone, clay, glass products	10	4.3	53.0
Heavy industry[a]	24	10.4	63.5
Services			
Travel, hotels, tourism	5	2.2	2.2
Transportation and storage	5	2.2	4.3
Communications[b]	3	1.3	5.7
Construction, civil engineering, architecture	4	1.7	7.4
Distribution[c]	56	24.3	31.7
Insurance	2	0.9	32.6
Computers[d]	4	1.7	34.3
Miscellaneous business (e.g., legal)	5	2.2	36.5
Total	230	100.0	

a. Primary and fabricated metal products, machinery and equipment, electronic equipment, transportation equipment, and other miscellanous manufacturing industries.

b. Service providers, courier, video production and distribution.

c. Wholesale and retail trade and franchising.

d. Software, systems design, data processing, and hardware maintenance and repair.

Table 4-3. *Estimated Trading Costs in the Arab Region*
by Type of Trading Activity

Percent

Trading activity	Range[a]	Share of total
Manufacturer and exporter	10–5	17
Manufacturer, importer, and exporter	8–10	33
Importer and distributor	8–10	20
Importer and exporter	5–10	16
Other	10–20	14
Weighted average trading cost		10.6

a. Percent of value of imports.

duties and domestic taxes, both of these were ranked as the most binding constraints (table 4-4). Moreover, the interviewed companies reported that although customs duties and other import charges have been reduced in most Arab countries, the reductions were being offset by increases in domestic taxes.

The questionnaire asked companies that dealt with import clearance and inspection questions about informal payments by traders to customs and other trade-related officials. The compiled results show that Arab companies in the sampled countries pay on average 1 percent of the value of imports as "additional payments" to customs officials. A large number of interviewed companies mentioned that these "irregular payments" are usu-

Table 4-4. *Costs of Trade Constraints, as Ranked by Arab Companies*

Constraint	Rank	Average score[a]	Standard deviation
Customs duties and other import charges	1	3.0	1.1
Domestic taxes	2	2.6	1.3
Customs clearance	3	2.5	1.1
Public sector corruption	4	2.4	1.4
Inspection/conformity certification	5	2.2	1.3
Transshipment regulatory measures	6	2.1	1.3
Business visa restrictions	7	1.8	1.5

a. Average scores for constraints were scaled from 4 (prohibitive) to 1 (not costly). Constraints with a score equal to or greater than 1.8 were retained in the final results.

Table 4-5. *Average "Additional Payments" to Customs Officials,*
by Country[a]

Percent

| | Additional payments as percent of import value | | | | | |
Country	0–1	2–9	10–17	18–25	>25	Don't know
Gaza-West Bank	92				8	
Egypt	33	12	3		3	48
Jordan	72	25				3
Lebanon	17	42	14	3		24
Saudi Arabia	33	33				33
Syria	41	42	8			9
Tunisia	77					23
UAE	82					18
Average	56.3	18.6	3.6	0.5	1	20

a. Values in table represent percent of companies reporting payments.

ally in kind. In addition, there was wide agreement among the companies that making additional payments is a common practice in most Arab countries; for instance, not a single company was exempt from additional payments for clearance of an import transaction in Lebanon and Syria. As shown in table 4-5, half of the responding companies in Lebanon and Syria estimated that typical additional payments to customs officials in their country ranged between 2 and 17 percent.

Another set of intangible costs that the questionnaire addressed are those associated with import and export procedures and requirements, namely the time constraints for import clearance and inspection; the number of documents and signatures required to process a trade transaction; and the number of workdays that a company spends in dealing with problems with customs and other government officials. The compiled results provide some estimates. For instance, it takes two to five days on average to release goods imported by air freight from customs; two to ten days for sea shipment; and one to three days for road shipment. In contrast, the norm is less than six hours to clear air freight, less than twenty-four hours to clear sea freight; and less than four hours to clear shipment by road. Another significant administrative cost highlighted in the survey involves the large number of

Table 4-6. *Number of Documents and Signatures Needed for Trade Transactions*

Type of transport	Number of documents		Number of signatures	
	Imports	Exports	Imports	Exports
Air freight	5	5	10–20	8–10
Sea freight	6	5	12–20	8–10
Road	5	5	11–15	11–15

documents and signatures required for processing a trade transaction. Table 4-6 shows that up to twenty signatures are needed, on average, to process an air or sea freight shipment.

Other administrative costs are entailed in the number of workdays a year that Arab companies spend in resolving problems with customs and other government officials. The compiled data show an estimated ninety-five workdays a year, although the mode (that is, the estimate for more than 50 percent of the respondents) is about thirty workdays a year. Moreover, about 10 percent of the respondents had daily contact (365 days a year) with customs and other government officials. Interviewed companies considered such daily contacts with government officials to be an inducement to corruption and a source of additional costs of trading. This may also explain the high ranking of the factor "public sector corruption" on the list of the most costly constraints perceived by Arab companies. The compiled results by country show that three countries spend more time than the regional average in dealing with customs and tax departments: traders in Egypt, Jordan, and Syria spent an average of 100, 200, and 209 workdays, respectively.

Finally, companies were asked whether difficulties in dealing with customs and other trade officials have decreased or increased in the last three years. The compiled results show that, on average, 41 percent of the respondents thought that the difficulties had decreased, 36 percent believed that they had remained about the same, and 15 percent believed that they had increased. Table 4-7 displays detailed responses to this question in each of the surveyed countries. The results suggest that on average the situation has improved in the region, especially in Egypt and Jordan.

Obstacles to establishing and operating a business in the service sector by national and foreign (other Arab) companies were addressed by asking the

Table 4-7. *Companies' Difficulty in Dealing with Customs and Tax Officials Today Compared with Three Years Ago, by Country*

Percent of country total

Country	Increased	Remained the same	Decreased	Don't know
Egypt	16	22	56	6
Gaza–West Bank	35	35	18	12
Jordan	5	26	63	7
Lebanon	17	50	31	3
Saudi Arabia	17	67	17	...
Syria	33	50	17	...
Tunisia	17	46	25	13
UAE	4	35	38	23
Average	15	36	41	9

sampled companies to judge how problematic laws and regulations governing service activities were. The responding companies mentioned business licensing procedures; state monopoly of certain activities (for example, insurance); exclusive agency laws; mandatory employment of nationals; and public corruption as the major obstacles to service activities in the Arab region. Other services- and investment-related issues frequently mentioned by surveyed firms included the need for a regional entity to insure and finance exports and imports; the absence of mechanisms to hedge against trade risk along the lines of the U.S. Ex-Im Bank or the French COFACE model; difficulties in obtaining visas; restrictions on access of foreign service providers; and requirements to have a local sponsor.

Regarding major constraints in the business environment in the Arab region, the respondents ranked as the primary obstacle weak legal systems that fail to ensure that the terms of business contracts are honored (table 4-8). That was followed by direct state intervention to protect exclusive agents by giving territorial distributors monopoly over imports; this practice was more prevalent in the Gulf countries. Government limits on ownership of real estate and of equities are ranked third and fourth. That was complemented by traders' concern about corruption, domestic red tape, and bad governance, which was ranked fifth. Less transparent and complex tax systems and para-tariffs were ranked sixth.

Table 4-8. *Most Restrictive Constraints in the Arab Business Environment, as Ranked by Companies*

Constraint	Rank
Enforcement of the legal system	1
Agency law restricting business to nationals	2
Prohibition on foreign ownership of real estate	3
Limits on foreign ownership of equities	4
Corruption, red tape, and bad governance	5
Tax system and fees	6

Intensity of Trade Barriers on a Bilateral Country Pair Basis

The questionnaire asked exporting companies to judge the relative intensity of trade barriers in other Arab countries on a bilateral country pair basis. Compiled results identify a group of five Arab countries that were judged problematic by the interviewed companies and ranked the highest: Gaza–West Bank, Syria, Egypt, Tunisia, and Saudi Arabia (table 4-9).

The interviewed companies cited a number of reasons for their responses. Among the frequently cited reasons for Gaza–West Bank, the first on the list of problematic countries, were "border closure, restriction by Israeli government, Israeli cross-border restrictions." Syria was ranked second; some of the reasons cited were "bureaucracy, complex trade laws, lack of banking services to open letters of credit for Syrian importers, and corruption." Egypt was ranked third by the interviewed companies, which judged the Egyptian market to be "highly protected by high customs duties, import prohibition, product standards, unclear conformity certification procedure, and red tape." Tunisia ranked fourth. Reported reasons included "complex trade laws and directives, high customs duties, product inspection at the border takes too long, and government subsidies to Tunisian exporters for air transportation, insurance." Saudi Arabia was ranked fifth, for reasons such as "Saudi visa restrictions for business visits, local agency law that allows Saudi nationals only to register for business and to be an agent of a foreign company, Saudi customs bias against Arab-made products but easier access to Saudi markets for Asian, North American, and European products."

Table 4-9. *Trade Barriers in the "Most Problematic" Arab Countries, as Ranked by Companies*

Percent of country total

Country	High	Medium	Low	Mean[a]	Rank
Gaza–West Bank	52.5	33.9	13.6	2.0	1
Syria	31.7	49.2	19.0	2.1	2
Egypt	30.0	46.3	23.8	2.41	3
Tunisia	28.6	52.3	19.0	2.43	4
Saudi Arabia	16.4	51.0	32.7	2.8	5

a. Weighted average. Countries are ranked by mean score on a scale from 1 (extremely problematic) to 4 (not problematic).

Effectiveness of Trade Agreements

Interviewed companies were asked whether trade agreements signed by their respective governments with other Arab countries and foreign countries benefited their business; which of the trade agreements benefited their businesses the most; and in what way agreements worked in favor of their growth.

About half of the respondents replied that they had not benefited from any of the trade agreements signed by their governments with foreign countries. For the half that had benefited, the most beneficial trade agreements were the pan-Arab trade agreements such as bilateral protocols and the Greater Arab Free Trade Agreement (GAFTA). World Trade Organization (WTO) agreements came second, followed by the Gulf Cooperation Council (GCC) economic agreement and the Euro-Med free trade agreement. According to companies' responses, these agreements seem to work most in lowering tariffs and in providing companies with preferential access to exports. Of the Euro-Med agreements, companies in Tunisia and Morocco cited as the most favorable the "mise à niveau" (restructuring) program supported by the EU for Mediterranean partner countries. Those who replied that they had not benefited from the trade agreements cited many obstacles, some of which can be summarized as follows:

—Knowledge or awareness of the benefits of the agreements is lacking.

—Government agencies do not make enough effort to inform the public about the benefits of the agreements.

—Competition from Asian countries is much stronger, offsetting the benefits of the agreements.

—Implementation problems: partner countries do not commit to terms and conditions of the agreements; the articles of some agreements are left to the interpretation of customs officials, who lack knowledge about the operations of the agreements.

—Trade agreements do not reduce the numerous administrative procedures, paperwork, and red tape.

—Implementation of certain articles of the agreements is not reciprocal.

—Transportation between Arab countries is inadequate.

Business Environment for Direct Intraregional Investment

The questionnaire included a module for respondents representing companies that had made or were thinking of making a direct investment in other Arab countries. The questions asked what Arab investors thought about intraregional foreign direct investment (FDI) and asked them to rank the most important factors in FDI decisions. The compiled responses show that investors ranked the following factors as extremely important: ability to repatriate capital; political stability; predictability and reliability; size of the domestic market; and legal system to enforce contract.

Summary and Conclusion

This survey is a major attempt to quantify the costs of complying with administrative and related sources of trading costs in eight Arab countries. Trading costs are the less transparent barriers to trade such as customs procedures, restrictions on overland transport and transit, product standards and certifications of conformity, competition policy, and political barriers. The main findings can be recapitulated as follows. First, although tariffs and other taxes on imports have been declining in most Arab countries in recent years, Arab companies still perceive tariffs and domestic taxes to be relatively high and to exceed nontariff trading costs.[2] Moreover, customs duties tend to be compounded by the costs of complying with regulations and administrative constraints, which have been estimated by 230 randomly

2. Zarouk (2000).

selected companies in eight Arab countries to range between 8 and 10 percent of the value of trade.

The survey also showed that a typical sea freight import transaction in Arab countries takes two to ten days to clear, whereas the norm is less than twenty-four hours. A truck delivering goods to market across any two Arab countries may take one to three days to clear, whereas the norm is four hours. Moreover, an average Arab company spends ninety-five workdays per year—more than one week a month—in resolving problems with customs and other trade officials. Such daily contact with government officials represents an additional trading cost and an inducement to corruption in the form of customs officials' demands for informal payments. Arab companies estimate these additional payments to represent 1 percent of the costs of delivered goods.

In recent years, most Arab countries have made efforts to reduce traditional trade barriers such as tariffs and quantitative restrictions on imports, in addition to reforming customs administration. The survey confirms those efforts, showing that 41 percent of respondents thought that difficulties in dealing with customs and other trade departments had receded in Arab countries, especially in Egypt and Jordan.

An effective approach to dealing with trading costs could be implemented in a regional context, through free trade agreements signed by Arab countries.[3] Such policy instruments may facilitate trade considerably, especially by eliminating redundant procedures and cross-border transportation restrictions. However, the survey shows that intra-Arab free trade agreements such as GAFTA seem to work best in lowering tariffs and providing exporting industries with preferential market access in other Arab countries. Therefore, such intraregional trade liberalization among Arab countries has not lowered the bureaucratic delays at the borders nor streamlined the domestic red tape and bad governance that remain costly and corrosive across Arab countries.

As the world moves toward trade regimes with very low tariffs, or indeed toward free trade, the removal of other barriers to trade, such as import quotas, import licensing, and technical barriers, also is under way under the WTO agreements. The real gains from intra-Arab regional agreements such

3. Zarrouk and Zallio (2001).

as GAFTA would be found in removing the administrative requirements that this survey has quantified and shown to raise significantly the cost of trading in the Arab region.

References

Hoekman, Bernard, and Patrick Messerlin. 2002. "Harnessing Trade for Development and Growth in the Middle East." New York: Council on Foreign Relations (www.cfr.org [November 6, 2002]).

Zarrouk, Jamel. 2000. "Para-tariff Measures in Arab Countries." In *Trade Policy Developments in the Middle East and North Africa*, edited by Bernard Hoekman and Kheir-El-Din. Washington: World Bank.

Zarrouk, Jamel, and Franco Zallio. 2001. "Integrating Free Trade Agreements in the Middle East and North Africa." *Journal of World Investment* 2 (June 2001): 403–26.

5

Alternative Paths to Prosperity: Economic Integration among Arab Countries

DENISE EBY KONAN

Recent events have thrust Middle Eastern political relations into the world spotlight once again. Clearly, economic prosperity and the alleviation of poverty and unemployment would go far to ease regional political unrest, and to that end negotiations to enhance Arab economic cooperation have been accelerated. Social and political transformations that are well underway in key Arab countries also are enhancing prospects for economic transformation. For example, recent transfers of leadership in Algeria, Jordan, Morocco, Bahrain, and Syria suggest the potential for greater openness to trade. Policy reforms in many countries in the region also reflect a greater willingness to engage in the world economy.

Just as regional peace has remained elusive, the regional economy has failed to live up to the promise of the significant macroeconomic policy reforms undertaken by several Arab countries. Beginning in the mid-1980s, Jordan, Algeria, Morocco, Tunisia, and Egypt implemented extensive, largely

The author thanks Bernard Hoekman, Jamel Zarrouk, Keith Maskus, and Joe Francois for their valuable input. Helpful comments were provided by Hanaa Kheir-El-Din, Ali Soliman, and others. The research assistance of Tu Ha also is gratefully acknowledged, as is financial support from the Council on Foreign Relations.

unilateral, economic policy reforms.[1] Trade reform measures generally began with streamlining the tariff system and lowering the effective rate of protection. While the economic reform packages were somewhat successful in stimulating economies, GDP growth in the region has only roughly kept pace with population growth. Inadequate growth rates are particularly problematic when combined with a work force that is young and an employment rate that is high in comparison with world averages. The social fabric would benefit greatly from meaningful employment opportunities for new workers.

Enhancement of Arab economic prosperity is a regional rather than country-specific issue because of several factors. First, as recognized by Robert Z. Lawrence, multilateral reform efforts such as those embodied in the World Trade Organization (WTO) tend most readily to achieve liberalization of the transparent border barriers—"shallow integration".[2] Globalization, however, increasingly places pressure on countries to harmonize regulatory and administrative barriers—"deep integration." Lawrence observes that deep integration is more likely to be achieved when negotiated on a bilateral or regional basis than in multilateral forums such as the WTO.

Second, labor markets within Arab countries are marked by rather significant regional links. As Galal points out, there is a substantial intraregional flow of workers' remittances to Yemen, Jordan, Egypt, and the Palestinian Authority, primarily from oil-exporting economies.[3] Given demographic patterns and a young work force, unemployment becomes a regional issue rather than a purely national one. Finally, economies are places, and location matters. The geographic landscape of the Middle East and North Africa generally requires that nations cooperate on economic issues in order to trade with the rest of the world. Cooperation in building regional synergies in infrastructure, allocation of natural resources, and labor mobility as well as policy harmonization provides the opportunity to unify what now are small and fragmented economies.

This chapter attempts to assess alternative strategies for achieving economic prosperity in representative Arab countries. Due to the availability of data and well-established models, the focus is on the economies of Egypt and Tunisia. Potential costs and benefits from economic integration were

1. See Nabli and De Kleine (2000) for further discussion.
2. Lawrence (1996).
3. Galal (2000).

calculated by using computable general equilibrium models of the two economies. The analysis considers not only shallow integration scenarios but also the possibility for deeper integration through coordination of regulatory procedures and liberalization of barriers to trade in services.

Trade liberalization has been a prominent component of government reform in Egypt and Tunisia. Both countries have been reducing tariffs significantly since the 1980s. Both are signatories to the World Trade Organization, and both also have entered into separate bilateral agreements with the European Union.[4] In each country, there have been preliminary discussions about possible trade agreements with the United States, although no formal agreements have been reached.[5] A wide literature has likewise emerged on each of these initiatives.

In this context, it is perhaps surprising that integration efforts within the region have been lackluster and the economic implications of greater Arab cooperation less explored. In the case of Egypt, there has been some preliminary exploration of effects. Hoekman and Konan consider trade opportunities for Egypt in the context of an EU agreement, an Arab agreement, and unilateral most favored nation (MFN) liberalization.[6] As demonstrated in this chapter, a shallow integration agreement with either the EU or Arab countries generates little welfare gain, reflecting the fact that Egypt already has duty-free access to much of the EU and that such an agreement would lead to trade diversion.[7] Substantial welfare gains depend on the elimination of regulatory, administrative, and other nontariff barriers (NTBs). The actual impact will depend heavily on several factors. The first is the degree to which barriers would be liberalized on a nondiscriminatory basis. That is, deeper integration with the EU may assist Egypt in developing more streamlined regulatory measures that are in line with international standards and therefore may ease trade restrictions with countries outside of the EU. Another important issue is whether barriers generate rents or are largely frictional; the latter generates the greatest potential gain from liberalization.

---

4. Galal and Hoekman (1997) explore the possible implications of the Euro-Mediterranean agreements, with an emphasis on Egypt.

5. See Galal and Lawrence (1998) and Hoekman, Konan, and Maskus (1998) for further discussion.

6. Hoekman and Konan (2000, 2001).

7. See Konan and Maskus (1997, 2002b), for a discussion of bilateral trade patterns and the Egypt-EU Agreement. As Egypt trade is not heavily concentrated with the EU, a shallow agreement may lead to significant trade diversion.

An alternative to focusing on regional goods trade would be for Arab countries to integrate service markets into the global economy. This option is especially attractive as the benefits are likely to be substantial. Services have become an increasingly important component of economic activity, and yet they have remained highly regulated and protected from international competition in both Egypt and Tunisia. More recently, services also have become the subject of intensive multilateral negotiation in the context of the General Agreement on Trade in Services (GATS) of the World Trade Organization. Unlike trade in goods, trade in services involves modes of delivery beyond cross-border exchange, such as the movement of personnel and consumers and the presence of foreign subsidiaries.

In a computable general equilibrium (CGE) model of Tunisia, Konan and Maskus consider both goods and services liberalization, finding that gains from services liberalization, including cross-border as well as foreign investment, significantly outweigh those from goods liberalization.[8] The lion's share of the gains comes from the reduction of barriers to foreign direct investment in the service sector. As is expected, goods trade liberalization tends to reorient production and the work force toward manufacturing and raise wages relative to returns to capital. In contrast, services liberalization results in more balanced growth with far less movement of factors across sectors and more even distribution of increases in returns to factors. This chapter builds on that methodology and extends the analysis to Egypt.

To summarize, Arab countries may elect to integrate more fully with the global economy through several channels. Regional negotiations may lower tariff barriers as well as important regulatory and other nontariff barriers to trade in goods. Alternatively, efforts to liberalize service sector trade could be pursued. The resulting impacts on economic activity depend in important ways on which paths are chosen. Those impacts differ in Egypt and Tunisia, owing to important structural differences in the underlying composition of economic activities. It is these impacts that this chapter explores.

Benchmark and Barriers: The Scope for Regional Integration

Table 5-1 presents an overview of Arab integration into the world economy relative to that of other regions. Jordan, Kuwait, Oman, Saudi Arabia,

8. Konan and Maskus (2002a).

Table 5-1. *Integration of Arab Economies in the Global Economy*
Percent of GDP, PPP

	Merchandise trade		Gross private capital flow		Gross foreign direct investment	
	1986	1996	1986	1996	1986	1996
Country						
Algeria	17.3	15.0	0.8	n.a.	0.0	n.a.
Egypt	13.6	14.8	4.6	2.5	1.5	0.4
Jordan	36.8	36.6	3.3	4.7	0.4	0.4
Kuwait	54.3	45.8	41.1	16.8	1.0	1.7
Libya	n.a.	n.a.	n.a.	n.a.	n.a.	n.a.
Morocco	12.6	14.0	2.8	1.7	0.0	0.4
Oman	52.9	45.4	10.2	2.5	1.4	0.2
Saudi Arabia	36.2	41.2	14.2	5.5	0.9	1.0
Syria	20.0	19.6	6.1	5.0	0.0	0.2
Tunisia	20.6	30.2	3.8	5.8	0.3	0.6
UAE	83.6	135.7	n.a.	n.a.	n.a.	n.a.
Income group						
Low	7.1	7.9	2.0	2.1	0.2	1.0
Middle	12.5	21.8	4.0	5.8	0.3	0.9
High	26.5	38.9	11.4	19.3	1.6	2.7
Low- and middle-income by region						
East Asia and Pacific	9.1	13.0	1.7	1.9	0.2	1.0
Europe and Central Asia	n.a.	25.5	n.a.	9.2	n.a.	0.8
Latin America and Caribbean	7.9	17.3	4.6	6.6	0.3	1.1
Arab countries	19.4	18.9	5.0	3.2	0.4	0.4
South Asia	4.9	5.8	1.2	0.9	0.0	0.2
Sub-Saharan Africa	15.8	18.9	4.8	5.7	0.3	0.4

Source: Nabli and De Kleine (2000) and World Bank, *World Development Indicators,* 1998.

Tunisia, and the United Arab Emirates (UAE) are open, with merchandise trade as a share of real gross domestic product exceeding 30 percent and as much as 135 percent in oil-rich UAE. In contrast, goods markets in Egypt and Morocco appear to be relatively closed, with merchandise trade shares of 10 to 15 percent of real GDP. As a group, Arab countries have lagged behind those in other regions in the rate and depth of global integration. Note that the ratio of merchandise trade to GDP actually fell for the region between 1986 and 1996, as did the ratio of gross private capital flows to GDP.

Tariff Barriers and Shallow Integration

Many Arab countries maintain average tariff barriers that are above those found in most of the rest of the world. The unweighted average tariff in the region is around 19 percent and the trade-weighted applied tariff rate is somewhat lower at 15 percent (table 5-2). Although tariffs in the region are trending downward, they are doing so at a much slower rate than in East Asia and Latin America. There are clear differences in tariff structures across countries. Tariffs tend to be quite high in Egypt, Tunisia, and Morocco, with rates exceeding those of most of Latin America. Tariffs in most of the oil-exporting countries (with the exception of Saudi Arabia) are relatively low, reflecting a strong tradition of trade. Another important feature of trade policies is tariff escalation.[9] As shown in table 5-3, tariffs on raw materials are considerably lower than those on semiprocessed and final goods and certain protected agricultural and processed food items. Finally, para-tariffs are quite substantial in many Arab countries.[10]

Deep Integration: Regulatory Reform and Services Liberalization

A key to deep integration is the identification and removal of nontariff barriers. NTBs include import quotas, licensing and certification requirements, product standards, antidumping measures, customs procedures, and other regulatory and administrative barriers. As discussed in Galal and in Hoekman and Konan, NTBs act to segment markets, reduce competition, impose frictional costs that use real resources, and prohibit entry by foreign investors.[11]

NTBs typically are very difficult to document; however, survey work by Jamel Zarrouk provides extremely valuable documentation of Arab country NTBs and their effects.[12] Respondents reported that NTBs average 10 percent of the value of goods shipped and ranked customs clearance procedures, public sector corruption, and inspection/certification as imposing the highest trading costs.[13] In Egypt, for example, Kheir-El-Din reports that multiple centers of authority have led to a system in which delays and duplication of product testing are common and the inspection process overly

9. Zarrouk (2000c).
10. Zarrouk (2000b).
11. Galal (2000) and Hoekman and Konan (2000, 2001).
12. Zarrouk (2000a, 2000b, 2001).
13. See Zarrouk, chapter 4 of this volume.

Table 5-2. *Simple Average Tariff Rates by Region*

Percent

Region	1978–80	1981–1985	1986–90	1991–95	1996–99
Africa	38.2	29.3	26.9	22.3	17.8
East Asia	23.5	26.9	20.7	14.6	10.4
Latin America	28.1	26.4	24.1	13.9	11.1
Middle East[a]	29.6	24.6	24.1	22.9	19.3
South Asia	n.a.	71.9	69.8	38.9	30.7
Small states	29.8	33.9	16.9	17.2	12.9
Europe/Central Asia	12.0	21.6	14.9	8.1	10.1
Industrial economies	11.9	8.9	8.2	6.8	6.1

Source: World Bank.
a. Excluding members of OPEC.

labor intensive.[14] According to the Zarrouk survey, improvements in trading services appear to be slow, with 36 percent of respondents indicating that difficulties had not changed and 15 percent claiming that they had risen. Although tariff rates have been declining in many Arab countries, businesses still perceive trade and domestic barriers as being relatively high and a significant cost of trade.[15]

Liberalization of the service sector has become an area of intense regional and multilateral negotiation, the most prominent example being the ongoing discussions in the WTO. Because of data limitations and gaps in methodology, few empirical studies exist that examine the role that liberalization might play within developing countries. An important difference between trade in goods and trade in services is that, by definition, goods are physical and tangible and services often are intangible. Goods may be shipped across borders and because of their visibility easily regulated through taxes and customs procedures. In contrast, many service transactions involve personal contact between the provider and the client. While some, such as computer software services, may flow across borders, other international transactions require the movement of either the persons involved or the ownership of the firm in which a transaction is conducted. Thus GATS distinguishes between four "modes of supply": cross-border trade (mode 1); movement of consumers (mode 2); foreign investment (mode 3); and temporary movement of natural service providers (mode 4).

14. Kheir-El-Din (2000).
15. Zarrouk, this volume.

Table 5-3. Trade Tariffs and Nontariff Barriers

Percent

| | Primary products | | | | | Manufactures and other goods | | | | | |
	Food (SITC 0)	Beverages and tobacco (SITC 1)	Crude materials (SITC 2)	Mineral fuels (SITC 3)	Fats and oils (SITC 4)	Chemicals (SITC 5)	Material manufactures (SITC 6)	Machinery and equipment (SITC 7)	Miscellaneous manufactures (SITC 8)	Commodities and transactions not classified (SITC 9)	Year
Tariffs and paratariffs[a]											
Algeria	30.5	81.9	12.5	4.0	18.7	15.1	31.0	18.8	43.3	25.5	1993
Egypt	35.6	46.1	14.0	13.3	18.0	16.4	36.8	20.9	45.7	17.4	1995
Morocco	86.7	73.2	31.0	29.6	47.5	50.0	70.5	55.3	85.3	17.1	1993
Oman	7.1	69.3	5.5	3.9	1.9	5.1	5.3	5.0	5.0	4.2	1992
Saudi Arabia	10.2	12.6	11.8	12.0	12.0	11.9	12.3	12.0	12.7	11.0	1994
Tunisia	38.3	42.7	21.1	11.8	30.3	21.2	32.2	26.4	34.9	36.3	1995
Frequency of NTBs											
Algeria	96.6	66.7	0.0	0.0	61.2	1.0	2.0	0.0	0.0	0.0	1993
Tunisia	10.1	0.0	0.5	0.0	0.0	0.0	20.1	0.3	25.9	0.0	1992
Saudi Arabia	0.6	0.0	0.0	0.0	0.0	0.0	0.0	0.0	0.0	0.0	1995
Oman	0.0	48.1	3.9	0.0	0.0	3.1	0.3	2.5	5.0	0.0	1992

Source: United Nations Conference on Trade and Development (UNCTAD), *Trade Analysis and Information Systems*, version 3.0, Fall 1995 (CD-ROM).

a. Paratariffs are customs surcharges, internal taxes on imports, decreed customs values, and other charges levied on imports that increase the cost of imports in a manner similar to ordinary import tariff measures.

The Models and Benchmark Data

This section presents the theoretical structure of the Egypt and Tunisia CGE models and describes the benchmark data sets. Detailed descriptions of the base model and data sources are available on request; the equations are given in technical appendix 5A. In the case of Egypt, the base model is described in detail in Maskus and Konan and in Konan and Maskus.[16] The Tunisia model is presented in full detail in Konan and Maskus.[17]

Each model stands alone in the sense that Egypt and Tunisia both are assumed to be price takers on world markets. Production is characterized by constant returns to scale and perfect competition, implying that prices equal marginal costs of output. The nesting structure is given in figure 5-1.[18] In all sectors, production functions are approximated with Leontief technologies using intermediate inputs and real value added. Value added comprises labor and capital inputs, which are distinguished in production by a constant elasticity of substitution (CES) production function. In the case of Egypt, labor is further disaggregated into production and nonproduction labor.

Products are differentiated by country of origin according to the Armington assumption, so that export and import prices differ across regions.[19] In each sector, demand for domestically produced and imported goods is represented by a CES function, and intermediate imports also are differentiated by region of supply in a CES structure. Similarly, domestic industries supply regionally differentiated goods to both domestic and foreign markets (exports). Production follows a nested two-stage constant elasticity of transformation (CET) function. Total output is first calculated as the sum of domestic supply and total exports, with the latter then being allocated across regions—the EU, the Arab League, and the rest of the world

16. Maskus and Konan (1997); Konan and Maskus (1997).

17. Konan and Maskus (2002a).

18. Labor-capital substitution varies across sectors, ranging from 0.43 to 1.99, as taken from Harrison and others (1993) and reported in Maskus and Konan (1997) and Konan and Maskus (2002b). In the case of Egypt, the elasticity of substitution between production and nonproduction labor is assumed to be 0.5.

19. De Melo and Robinson (1989) show that models that allow product differentiation are well behaved under a small open economy assumption; in effect, the economy is a price taker at the level of aggregate trade flows, and each region's aggregation is sufficiently distinctive to support the Armington assumption.

Figure 5-1. *Nesting Structure of the CGE Models for Egypt and Tunisia*

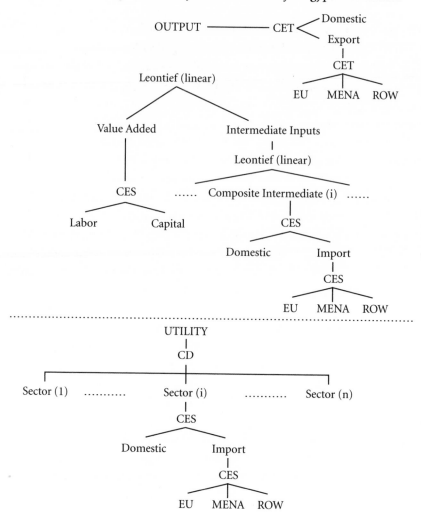

(ROW)—according to a sub-CET function. Capital is assumed to move freely across sectors, as is labor.[20]

A representative consumer maximizes a nested CES utility function with a corresponding multistaged budget constraint, shown in figure 5-1. In the

20. Benchmark trade elasticities are drawn from Rutherford, Rutstrom, and Tarr (2000). The various trade elasticities are 2.0 for substitution between domestic and imported goods,

first stage, the consumer decides how much to spend on goods from each sector, given the budget constraint. That is, the elasticity of substitution across sectors is unity, as given by a Cobb-Douglas (CD) utility nest. Given the sector-level expenditure decision, the consumer decides in stage two the domestic and aggregate imports in each sector according to a CES function. Then, given a budget for imports, the consumer selects purchases of imports from each region. The preferences of the government and investment agents are represented likewise.

The representative consumer receives income from primary factors (labor and capital), net transfers from the government, and the current account deficit. In addition, two standard closure rules are imposed: the savings-investment balance and a fixed current account balance. The savings-investment balance is based on the assumption that the capital stock is exogenously fixed at the benchmark level. This stock is financed through forced consumer saving that acts as a direct (lump-sum) tax. The interest rate (an index price of the composite capital stock) is endogenous and determined by factor demand conditions.

The current account is defined as the sum of the merchandise trade balance, the services balance, net foreign worker remittances, and (negative) net payments on foreign capital.[21] Foreign reserves are held constant so that the current account will be just offset by (negative of) the capital account, and this balance is held constant throughout the simulations. Income from foreign remittances less foreign capital payments enters as an exogenous addition to the representative agent's income. To hold the current account balance fixed while international prices are constant requires a balancing item. This is accomplished by means of a change in the home "real exchange rate," which refers implicitly to a change in the home price index (generated by changes in the price of home-produced goods) sufficient to sustain a current account balance as import and export volumes change.

International transactions also are assumed to encounter both tariffs and nontariff barriers. Tariff rates for Tunisia and Egypt are discussed below; the various sources and the role of NTBs are discussed in detail in Hoekman

---

5.0 for substitution among regional imports and for transformation between domestic output and exports, and 8.0 for transformation among regional export destinations.

21. In the 1995 benchmark year for Tunisia, foreign remittances were approximately 650 million dinars while net capital income totaled negative 680 million dinars (International Monetary Fund, 2000).

and Konan.[22] For the purposes of this analysis, NTBs are assumed to impose frictional costs on international transactions in both goods and services. That is, frictional NTBs employ resources in a wasteful manner and thus impose a cost on society. NTBs are directly unproductive and arise from excessive or redundant administrative procedures and regulations. It is recognized that costly administrative procedures are imposed by both the country itself (Tunisia and Egypt) and its Arab trading partners. Deep integration would thus involve a reduction of NTBs in Arab partner countries and lower the cost involved in exporting to the region.

No definitive measurements exist of the price-equivalent impact of NTBs, a problem that is not specific to Arab countries. The best information available comes from the survey work of Zarrouk, from which the benchmark NTBs for Egypt and Tunisia are taken.[23] It is assumed that frictional NTBs in agriculture and manufacturing impose an added cost of 15 percent on imports from Arab countries and 5 percent on imports from other trading partners. It is assumed that the Euro-Mediterranean agreement improves the price of exports to the EU by 5 percent in the apparel industry, 2 percent in agriculture, and 1 percent in other industries. Again, on the basis of the Zarrouk survey, the Greater Arab Free Trade Agreement is viewed as enhancing export prices of goods by 3 percent as regional tariff rates fall following shallow integration and by 15 percent due to a reduction of frictional barriers following deep integration.

In addition, barriers to foreign investment in the service sector are treated as driving a frictional wedge between the prices that would prevail in a liberalized environment and those in a distorted one. This follows the approach taken in Konan and Maskus in their modeling of service liberalization in Tunisia.[24] The present chapter adopts the Konan and Maskus technique of distinguishing between cross-border liberalization (mode 1 under GATS) and liberalization of investment barriers (mode 3). Barriers to cross-border trade in services tend to be administrative and regulatory in nature and raise the real cost of engaging in the transaction. Restrictions on foreign investment in the service sector (mode 3 barriers), in contrast, generally impede technology transfer and reduce competition, thus raising the

22. Hoekman and Konan (2000 and 2001).
23. Zarrouk (2001).
24. Konan and Maskus (2002a).

domestic cost of service provision above the cost that would prevail if world-class best practices were followed.

The government budget deficit is a deduction in available income for the representative agent, constituting a transfer to government consumption. The real expenditures of the government are held fixed during these simulations. Thus, if a policy reform causes prices to fall, thereby reducing the tax revenues required to finance government expenditures, the tax saving is transferred to the representative agent. At the same time, if trade liberalization results in lost tariff revenues, the revenues are recouped by allowing the primary tax instrument to vary proportionately. In the case of Tunisia, the endogenous tax instrument is the value-added tax. Egypt's revenue balance is achieved by allowing the goods and services tax rates to adjust. Tax instruments and their benchmark rates are discussed in the description of the data that follows. As shown in Konan and Maskus, the choice of replacement tax instrument interacts with trade policy liberalization in fundamental ways.[25]

The Tunisia Model and Benchmark Data

The data for the Tunisia model consist of a social accounting matrix (SAM) and other parameters, such as elasticities of substitution and transformation, import and export trade flows by region, and tax and tariff rates.[26] These data are assembled into a consistent set of relationships between intermediate demand, final demand, and value-added transactions using the 1995 input-output table for Tunisia provided by the Institut National de la Statistique (INS).[27] Production is disaggregated into thirty-six sectors as shown in table 5-4.

Tunisian production, column 1, tends to be concentrated in agriculture and fishing, processed foods (olive oil and dates), the apparel industry, and construction. Nearly 12 percent of output is in public services. Intra-industry trade in clothing and textiles is significantly high. With 21.5 percent of imports and 31.6 percent of exports, clothing and textile trade shares exceed those of all other sectors. Distortions in this sector are significant, with foreign investors producing largely for the export market and prohibited from

25. Konan and Maskus (2000).
26. See Konan and Maskus (2002a) for a detailed discussion of the Tunisia data and model.
27. The technique of data collection is described in Institut National de la Statistique (1998).

Table 5-4. *Sectoral Output and Trade Shares, Tunisia*
Percent

Sector	Production (1)	Imports (2)	Household consumption (3)	Intermediate consumption (4)	Exports (5)
Agriculture	7.66	7.12	10.83	11.77	1.57
Manufacturing					
Processed food	9.64	4.98	20.20	8.32	5.27
Ceramics and glass	3.16	1.25	0.51	6.34	1.53
Nonferrous metal	1.11	4.59	0.00	4.13	1.05
Metalwork	1.31	2.16	0.53	2.96	1.54
Machinery	0.35	10.39	0.5	1.85	0.82
Automobiles	0.88	6.49	3.71	1.51	.92
Automobile parts	0.06	1.08	0.02	0.06	0.09
Electrical parts	1.05	3.78	0.56	2.31	4.04
Electronics	0.63	3.63	1.06	1.08	0.94
Appliances	0.28	0.39	0.87	0.21	0.15
Chemicals	5.41	10.47	4.56	10.54	8.69
Clothing	9.90	21.52	8.43	11.85	31.59
Leather	1.47	1.73	2.24	1.14	3.17
Wood	1.57	1.49	2.28	2.28	0.18
Paper	1.19	2.44	0.85	3.10	0.63
Plastics	0.58	1.46	1.16	1.23	0.32
Other	0.48	1.89	1.18	0.65	1.35
Mining					
Mining	0.49	0.27	0.03	1.02	0.83
Petroleum	3.67	6.54	2.14	7.77	6.19
Utilities					
Electricity	1.71	0.02	1.14	1.86	n.t.
Water	0.43	n.t.	0.54	0.26	n.t.
Services					
Construction	7.19	n.t.	0.32	0.43	n.t.
Distribution	6.21	n.t.	0.00	0.00	n.t.
Transportation	5.15	3.24	5.44	4.35	8.98
Communication	0.98	0.11	0.28	1.69	0.37
Hotel	2.44	n.t.	3.73	0.10	n.t.
Restaurant	2.98	n.t.	10.41	0.03	n.t.
Finance	2.36	0.22	4.49	4.76	0.27
Insurance	0.33	0.25	0.27	0.58	0.02
Business	0.90	2.48	0.10	2.46	2.59
Real estate	0.33	0.01	4.77	1.35	0.01
Repair	0.95	n.t.	1.01	1.76	n.t.
Health	1.64	n.t.	4.72	0.22	n.t.
Public	11.71	n.t.	1.14	0.00	n.t.
Tourism	3.81	n.t.	n.t.	n.t.	16.87

Source: Institute National de la Statistique (1998).
n.t. = Not traded.

supplying the domestic market. Other important import sectors include machinery and chemicals, column 2. Exports are concentrated in apparel, tourism, and chemicals, which mostly go to the EU (table 5-5).

The main source of tax revenue in Tunisia is the value-added tax, which is applied on goods and services and on imports at rates ranging from zero to 29 percent. The standard tax rate was 17 percent for the 1995 benchmark and currently is 18 percent in response to tariff revenue losses anticipated with the EU agreement (see table 5-6 for benchmark rates). Trade and tariff data are aggregated to the input-output sectoral basis by using import weights using a concordance developed by the author. Tariff rates were determined by collections data for 1995 and vary across regions due to duty-drawback provisions as well as preferential treatment of the EU and the Arab League. There are no tariff collections on services, and their rates are assumed to be zero.

Table 5-6 provides the author's best estimate of price wedges resulting from service barriers. Mode 1 barriers on cross-border trade are treated as ad valorem tariff-equivalent NTBs. In regard to mode 3, it would be ideal to estimate the impact that services barriers have on both price markups and costs in order to distinguish between the competitive effect and the cost reduction effect of liberalization. In principle, the cost reduction effect could be captured by comparing actual costs to a constructed estimate of costs if services were provided according to a world-class best-practices cost function. Unfortunately, none of these measurements are attainable for Arab nations (or for most other countries).

The services barriers in table 5-6 are based on industry studies as well as on the survey work of Zarrouk; further discussion is provided in Konan and Maskus.[28] The estimates of financial services barriers are taken from the observation that the level of monetary intermediation in the banking system is about 30 percent lower than in comparable countries and on Goaied's estimation of the cost inefficiencies in the financial sector.[29] This is in line with the estimates of Kalirajan and others for the banking sectors in Chile, Singapore, South Korea, and Thailand.[30] The price wedges in insurance, communications, and transportation reflect the high level of benchmark

28. Zarrouk (2000a) and this volume; Konan and Maskus (2002a).
29. Goaied (1999).
30. Kalirajan and others (2000).

Table 5-5. *Benchmark Trade Shares, Tunisia*
Percent

Sector	Arab trade share		EU trade share	
	Imports	Exports	Imports	Exports
Agriculture and fishing	6.8	22.4	38.7	68.7
Manufacturing				
Processed food	4.0	12.5	55.3	71.9
Ceramics and glass	4.3	44.7	48.8	24.0
Nonferrous metal	36.4	25.7	57.7	70.4
Metalwork	4.3	28.9	67.8	58.8
Machinery	0.3	9.5	77.0	86.0
Automobiles and trucks	1.2	55.3	87.6	40.8
Automobile parts	0.0	28.8	57.1	71.0
Electrical parts	0.0	10.7	66.4	50.4
Electronics	0.0	10.7	66.4	50.4
Household appliances	0.0	10.7	66.4	50.4
Chemicals	3.1	18.3	75.7	39.2
Clothing and textiles	0.8	0.9	92.3	94.8
Leather	0.6	0.8	93.3	96.6
Wood	18.6	14.3	41.1	66.7
Paper	2.7	64.3	74.4	20.6
Plastics	13.8	57.9	72.9	28.0
Other manufacturing	0.1	9.5	72.9	76.2
Petroleum and mining				
Mining	33.5	2.1	30.6	86.0
Petroleum and gas	0.3	59.1	63.3	38.7
Services	5.0	9.0	70.0	76.0

Source: Konan and Maskus (2002a).

regulation in those sectors and comparisons with markets in similar countries.[31] The distribution and retail sectors are very fragmented and show large inefficiencies, making the 5 percent inefficiency measure quite conservative. Because many professional services are subject to a nationality requirement and thus restrict foreign participation, it is possible that the estimated price wedge is low. While the construction, engineering, and hotel service sectors are viewed as being largely liberalized, foreign participation is subject to investment codes.

31. World Bank (2000).

Table 5-6. *Benchmark Policy Parameters, Tunisia*

Ad valorem rates

| Sector | Trade-weighted tariffs | Services barriers | | Weighted VAT |
		Cross-border	Investment	
Agriculture	13.0			6.0
Manufacturing				
Processed food	18.5			21.4
Ceramics and glass	23.6			17.0
Nonferrous metal	21.2			17.0
Metalwork	17.5			17.0
Machinery	8.5			17.0
Automobiles	10.8			14.6
Automobile parts	1.7			17.5
Electrical parts	7.8			16.8
Electronics	7.8			16.8
Appliances	7.8			16.8
Chemicals	10.3			15.0
Clothing	21.6			22.3
Leather	28.3			17.0
Wood	16.6			17.0
Paper	5.3			17.0
Plastics	18.7			17.0
Other	15.8			15.1
Mining				
Mining	2.5			17.0
Petroleum	20.2			6.0
Utilities				
Electricity				6.0
Water				17.0
Services				
Construction		n.t.	3	17.0
Distribution		n.t.	5	0.0
Transportation		50	3	6.3
Communication		200	30	0
Hotel		n.t.	5	6.0
Restaurant		n.t.	5	6.0
Finance		30	30	6.0
Insurance		50	50	6.0
Business		10	10	6.0
Real Estate		10	10	6.0
Repairs		n.t.	3	6.0
Health		n.t.	3	6.0
Public		n.t.	3	6.0

Source: Data provided by the Tunisian Ministry of Finance.

n.t. = Nontraded mode of supply.

Table 5-7. *Benchmark Trade Shares, Egypt*

Percent

Sector	U.S. trade share		Arab trade share[a]		EU trade share[b]	
	Imports	Exports	Imports	Exports	Imports	Exports
Agriculture						
Vegetable, food	47.9	1.5	2.2	63.5	11.7	27.0
Vegetable, nonfood	16.5	13.4	1.2	14.1	36.9	49.3
Animal	0.0	2.3	9.6	53.0	82.7	35.2
Mining						
Petroleum	7.0	4.6	24.4	1.0	52.0	30.6
Mining	14.8	9.2	3.5	21.4	17.7	56.8
Manufacturing						
Food processing	10.6	4.5	2.3	49.3	40.3	20.1
Beverages	16.3	0.0	28.5	87.6	41.7	1.2
Tobacco	27.4	0.7	2.5	45.3	27.0	0.4
Cotton ginning	0.3	0.2	0.9	1.4	36.9	33.7
Cotton spinning	7.1	10.9	3.7	6.1	33.4	72.4
Clothing	0.9	49.1	19.1	8.6	12.4	34.7
Leather	0.9	1.5	13.8	30.9	25.7	48.8
Shoes	2.9	1.9	12.0	60.5	16.0	20.5
Wood	1.4	0.1	0.4	86.1	39.8	1.5
Furniture	34.7	10.6	1.4	58.5	57.0	14.9
Paper	17.1	0.8	2.9	91.7	46.8	1.6
Chemicals	12.2	3.5	7.9	39.4	62.6	31.3
Petroleum refining	6.2	0.6	28.9	7.2	48.4	58.5
Rubber, plastics	20.4	0.7	9.8	45.3	42.8	41.3

(continued)

The Egypt Model and Benchmark Data

The Egypt model is developed from a social accounting matrix for the Egyptian economy for 1994. The model was benchmarked to the 1990 input-output table for Egypt and updated to 1994 by using proprietary trade and tariff data, in a process described in Maskus and Konan (see table 5-7).[32] Production is disaggregated into thirty-eight sectors, including agriculture, mining, manufacturing, and services, as shown in table 5-8. Note in column 1 that the largest output shares are in vegetable food products, animal

32. Maskus and Konan (1997).

Table 5-7. *Benchmark Trade Shares, Egypt (Continued)*

Percent

Sector	U.S. trade share		Arab trade share[a]		EU trade share[b]	
	Imports	Exports	Imports	Exports	Imports	Exports
Porcelain	7.8	1.5	11.5	32.4	47.4	42.2
Glass	5.3	5.5	3.6	62.1	63.3	9.3
Minerals[c]	3.8	2.0	2.2	80.9	61.6	4.8
Base metals	11.8	1.9	9.0	24.3	35.5	68.3
Machinery	17.4	3.9	2.4	58.0	59.4	9.5
Transportation	12.1	0.3	0.7	89.8	33.8	3.6
Other	11.2	3.2	3.5	62.5	47.6	25.4
Services						
Utilities	16.8	7.0	4.3	40.0	44.6	25.0
Construction	16.8	7.0	4.3	40.0	44.6	25.0
Trade	16.8	7.0	4.3	40.0	44.6	25.0
Restaurant, hotel	16.8	7.0	4.3	40.0	44.6	25.0
Transportation	16.8	6.7	4.3	20.2	44.6	44.7
Communications	16.8	7.0	4.3	40.0	44.6	25.0
Finance	16.8	7.0	4.3	40.0	44.6	25.0
Insurance	16.8	7.0	4.3	40.0	44.6	25.0
Real estate	16.8	7.0	4.3	40.0	44.6	25.0
Social	16.8	7.0	4.3	40.0	44.6	25.0
Recreational	16.8	7.0	4.3	40.0	44.6	25.0
Personal	16.8	7.0	4.3	40.0	44.6	25.0

Source: Maskus and Konan (1997).
a. Excluding Israel.
b. Including Turkey.
c. Not elsewhere included.

products, food processing, trade, transport, social services, construction, and cotton textiles. Despite their relatively large presence in production, vegetable foodstuffs and food processing are major import goods, as are machinery and chemicals, as indicated in column 2. Egypt's export flows are dominated by transport services (due to the Suez Canal), oil, and textiles.

The policy framework facing Egypt is presented in table 5-9 and discussed at greater length in Maskus and Konan.[33] In 1990 Egypt levied indirect taxes and subsidies on production but modified this tax structure considerably by 1993, phasing in a new goods and services tax (GST) and

33. Maskus and Konan (1997).

Table 5-8. *Sectoral Output and Trade, Egypt*

Sectoral shares (percent)

Sector	Production	Imports	Exports
Agriculture			
Vegetable, food	12.4	13.3	2.6
Vegetable, nonfood	1.7	0.0[a]	0.1
Animal	8.0	0.8	0.3
Mining			
Petroleum	2.7	1.2	18.5
Mining	0.09	2.0	0.2
Manufacturing			
Food processing	7.7	15.1	1.3
Beverages	0.6	0.0[a]	0.0[a]
Tobacco	1.9	1.0	0.0[a]
Cotton ginning	1.2	0.5	4.2
Cotton spinning	5.2	2.4	10.3
Clothing	1.4	0.0[a]	1.2
Leather	0.2	0.0[a]	0.1
Shoes	0.4	0.0[a]	0.0[a]
Wood	1.1	5.0	0.1
Furniture	1.4	0.0	0.5
Paper	1.5	3.3	0.9
Chemicals	3.1	10.8	1.8
Petroleum refining	2.7	1.2	3.3
Rubber, plastics	0.8	2.3	0.3

(continued)

phasing out indirect production taxes and subsidies. The GST, which is applied on sales of goods and services at various rates, has a complicated structure. The rates, listed in column 1, vary from zero on food products, paper, petroleum refining, and insurance to 25 percent on many luxury and investment goods, such as machinery and transport equipment. The standard tax rate is 10 percent. Effective corporate tax rates on capital use are listed in column 2. There is no tax on agriculture, a 23 percent effective tax on services, and an 18 percent tax on manufactures.

Table 5-9 also reports 1994 tariff rates aggregated to the input-output basis. Egypt does not realize the full revenue from its legislated tariffs because of various exemptions for duty-drawback provisions, investment incentives, and performance requirements. The weighted legal tariff rates

Table 5-8. *Sectoral Output and Trade, Egypt (Continued)*

Sectoral shares (percent)

Sector	Production	Imports	Exports
Porcelain	0.3	0.4	0.1
Glass	0.3	0.5	0.1
Minerals[b]	1.7	0.4	0.0[a]
Base metals	2.8	2.6	0.8
Machinery	3.5	23.1	4.6
Transportation equipment	1.0	5.9	0.4
Other	0.1	0.5	0.1
Services			
Utilities	1.7	0.2	0.7
Construction	5.5	0.2	0.8
Trade	7.1	0.3	5.6
Restaurants/hotels	2.3	0.0	5.0
Transportation	6.0	1.3	31.9
Communications	0.8	0.1	0.4
Finance	1.5	1.1	n.t.
Insurance	0.3	n.t.	0.5
Real estate	2.8	3.9	n.t.
Social	6.0	0.1	0.2
Recreational	0.5	0.2	3.2
Personal	0.9	n.t.	n.t.

Source: Maskus and Konan (1997).
n.t. = Not traded.
a. Share is less than 0.005 percent.
b. Not elsewhere included.

are scaled down approximately 20 percent in order to be consistent with total import duty collections in 1994. As discussed above, the services estimates are those of the author and they are based in part on the Zarrouk surveys presented in this volume as well as on industry reviews.

Alternative Paths to Prosperity

This section presents an array of scenarios illustrating various types of liberalization of trade in goods and services. Preferential liberalization through either the Euro-Med initiative or the Greater Arab Free Trade Agreement and multilateral liberalization are explored. Levels of liberalization of trade in goods range from shallow integration, involving only tariffs on goods, to

Table 5-9. *Policy Parameters, Egypt*

Ad valorem rates

Sector	Goods and services tax, 1994	Capital tax, 1994	Egypt tariff, 1994	Arab tariff, 1994	Services barriers	
					Border	Investment
Agriculture						
Vegetable, food	0.0	0.0	2.5	6.3		
Vegetable, nonfood	10.0	0.0	6.7	28.9		
Animal	0.0	0.0	4.4	6.7		
Mining						
Petroleum	0.0	18.0	8.2	2.9		
Mining	10.0	18.0	7.0	15.6		
Manufacturing						
Food processing	0.0	18.0	6.8	18.3		
Beverages	10.0	18.0	953.2	14.8		
Tobacco	10.0	18.0	65.5	83.1		
Cotton ginning	10.0	18.0	17.3	24.9		
Cotton spinning	10.0	18.0	23.3	17.4		
Clothing	10.0	18.0	53.7	32.5		
Leather	10.0	18.0	34.8	44.6		
Shoes	10.0	18.0	51.8	36.9		
Wood	5.0	18.0	8.1	28.1		
Furniture	10.0	18.0	46.9	34.9		
Paper	0.0	18.0	13.3	18.6		
Chemical	5.0	18.0	8.9	17.6		
Petroleum refining	0.0	18.0	7.1	20.0		
Rubber, plastics	10.0	18.0	15.6	24.7		

(continued)

deep integration, in which NTBs to trade in goods are eliminated. Finally, the role of liberalization of trade in services is considered, including the reduction of barriers on cross-border trade as well as barriers to foreign direct investment in the service sector.

Shallow Integration Implies Small Returns

Several interesting observations follow from a trade liberalization exercise that involves only the elimination of tariff rates, either on a preferential or multilateral basis; the results are shown in table 5-10. It should be noted that

Table 5-9. *Policy Parameters, Egypt (Continued)*

Ad valorem rates

Sector	Goods and services tax, 1994	Capital tax, 1994	Egypt tariff, 1994	Arab tariff, 1994	Services barriers Border	Services barriers Investment
Porcelain	10.0	18.0	43.5	21.3		
Glass	10.0	18.0	29.6	17.2		
Minerals[a]	5.0	18.0	18.1	12.7		
Base metals	10.0	18.0	17.2	32.6		
Machinery	25.0	18.0	17.9	19.9		
Transportation	25.0	18.0	41.2	56.6		
Other	10.0	18.0	19.3	24.9		
Services						
Utility	2.5	23.0			n.t.	n.t.
Construction	10.0	23.0			3	3
Trade	8.0	23.0			6	5
Restaurants/hotels	8.0	23.0			3	5
Transportation	0.0	23.0			50	3
Communications	5.0	23.0			150	15
Finance	8.0	23.0			3	30
Insurance	0.0	23.0			n.t.	30
Real estate	8.0	23.0			10	10
Social	10.0	23.0			3	15
Recreational	8.0	23.0			3	3
Personal	10.0	23.0			n.t.	10

Source: Maskus and Konan (1997), Hoekman and Konan (2001).
n.t. = Nontraded modes of supply.
a. Not elsewhere included.

welfare is measured in equivalent variation terms and thus provides a real utility-based measure of the gains for households.

One of the most surprising results is that, with one exception, the gain from liberalization for Tunisia is significantly greater in percentage terms than that for Egypt. Trade liberalization involving the EU would raise Tunisian welfare, measured in terms of equivalent variation (EV) in household income, from 2.12 to 3.03 percent. GDP would increase from 4.23 to 5 percent, depending on the nature of the agreement. Due to deleterious trade diversion, a pure Greater Arab Free Trade Agreement would actually

Table 5-10. *Impact of Shallow Reform Scenarios, Tariffs Only*

	Euro-Med Agreement (SEU)	GAFTA (SME)	GAFTA + Euro-Med (SEM)	Most favored nation (SHA)	Euro-Med + GAFTA + MFN (SHM)
Tunisia					
Macroeconomic variables (percent change)					
Welfare (EV)	3.03	−0.07	3.02	2.12	2.20
GDP	5.00	−0.02	5.01	4.23	4.31
Consumer price index	−2.94	0.07	−2.93	−2.08	−2.15
Wage	7.02	−0.17	6.98	3.20	3.41
Price of other value added	−0.52	0.01	−0.52	0.67	0.64
Value added tax	0.19	0.01	0.20	0.29	0.29
Labor adjustment	5.49	0.15	5.46	1.62	1.77
Other value added adjustment	5.64	0.14	5.62	2.37	2.45
Production (share of GDP)					
Agriculture (19.5%)[a]	15.92	19.47	15.89	19.16	18.40
Manufacturing (33%)[a]	42.63	32.69	42.63	33.68	36.53
Mining and utilities (7%)[a]	5.76	7.23	5.91	6.53	6.11
Services excluding tourism (41%)[a]	35.69	40.61	35.57	40.62	38.95

Egypt

Macroeconomic variables (percent change)

Welfare (EV)	0.01	0.18	0.03	0.56	0.57
GDP	0.90	2.05	0.85	0.45	0.45
Consumer price index	-3.59	-3.75	-3.61	-4.11	-4.12
Wage production labor	1.67	2.22	1.71	1.81	1.82
Wage nonproduction labor	2.38	2.17	2.44	3.18	3.21
Price of other value added	1.80	1.87	1.82	2.21	2.21
Goods and services tax	-8.49	-43.95	-6.61	15.51	15.52
Production labor adjustment	1.09	0.45	1.16	1.95	1.97
Nonproduction labor adjustment	0.88	0.26	0.93	1.55	1.57
Other value added adjustment	1.09	0.53	1.13	1.90	1.91

Production (share of GDP)

Agriculture (22.6%)[a]	21.12	21.17	21.02	21.03	21.07
Manufacturing (39.8%)[a]	40.96	41.73	40.85	40.24	40.02
Mining and utilities (3.7%)[a]	3.81	3.56	3.77	3.88	3.82
Services excluding tourism (33.4%)[a]	34.11	33.54	34.36	34.84	35.09

Source: Author's calculations.

a. Benchmark figure.

lower Tunisian welfare. In contrast, static gains from shallow trade liberalization in Egypt are estimated at less than 1 percent. A shallow Egypt-EU trade agreement would have a negligible impact on the economy.

Counterfactual experiments (not shown) verified the following. First, the weighted average tariff rates in the benchmark are surprisingly similar for Egypt and Tunisia and do not explain the differences. Second, the dispersion of tariff rates across sectors is likewise not an explanation as remarkably similar results would emerge if benchmark tariff rates were uniform in each country and across all sectors. Third, Egypt's domestic tax structure, which has more domestic tax instruments and less uniformity of rates within instruments, is far more complicated than that of Tunisia. Yet the difference continues to hold even if all domestic tax instruments are replaced with a lump-sum tax.

The explanation appears to be differences in the openness of Tunisia and Egypt that are not attributable to tariff or tax policy. Tunisia's economy relies much more on trade than Egypt's does. In 1996, merchandise trade as a percentage of GDP on a purchasing power parity basis was 15 percent in Egypt and 30 percent in Tunisia (table 5-1). In terms of openness, Tunisia is similar to Saudi Arabia, Oman, Kuwait, and Jordan. With the exception of services, imported products are important in most sectors, while exports are concentrated in a few key sectors (table 5-4). Egypt's somewhat closed trade environment is comparable to that of Algeria, Morocco, and Syria. As shown in table 5-8, the relative volume of imports to Egypt are trivial in several key manufacturing sectors. What the data do not clearly show is why Egyptian markets are less reliant on international trade than those of Tunisia. There are several theoretical explanations. The Egyptian economy may be naturally somewhat self-sufficient (as is the United States, whose openness index is even lower). Egyptian trade transactions costs may be high in ways that are not as readily measurable. The infrastructure supporting trade—in communications, banking, or transportation, for example—might be inadequate. Egyptian consumers might have a greater preference for domestically produced goods than do Tunisian consumers. The regulatory and administrative transactions costs may be substantially higher in Egypt. Regardless of the cause, it is apparent that it will be much more difficult for Egypt than for Tunisia to gain from integration of any sort. Tariff barriers are far easier to change than the systemic elements that might be suppressing Egypt's volume of trade.

A second surprising result is the ranking of gains for Tunisia. Tunisia's welfare is actually lower if tariffs are lowered on a multilateral basis, even if the concessions in terms of access to European and regional markets are preserved (column SHM in table 5-10). The explanation for this counterintuitive result relies on the interaction between domestic taxes and trade taxes, an issue that is discussed at length in Konan and Maskus.[34] Throughout these scenarios, changes in tariffs and other policies are assumed to be revenue neutral, with domestic tax instruments changing to compensate for any rise or fall in tariff revenues. In the case of Tunisia, the instrument is a value added tax, and the tax rate differs across sectors (see table 5-6). Eliminating tariffs on a most favored nation basis creates greater stress on government revenues and requires a slightly higher percentage increase in the value added tax (VAT). Counterfactual experiments (not shown) verify that if a less distortionary tax instrument were available to Tunisia, gains from shallow integration would be uniformly higher. With an endogenous lump-sum tax, welfare from the shallow Euro-Med initiative would increase by 4.3 percent (GDP by more than 7 percent) and from MFN liberalization by more than 5 percent (GDP by 9 percent). In the case of Tunisia, relying on the primary domestic tax instrument significantly mitigates the gains from trade liberalization.

A third observation is that trade shares matter when considering regional integration. In the case of Tunisia, most of the gains from trade can be achieved through the Euro-Med initiative because Tunisia's trade is concentrated with Europe. Indeed, given the loss of tax revenues and the lack of nondistortionary alternative instruments, an MFN initiative might yield lower welfare levels than a preferential agreement. Given the rather small volume of benchmark trade with regional countries, Tunisia would actually lose from a purely Arab-focused trade agreement due to trade diversion. In contrast, trading patterns in Egypt are diverse, and they include a substantial volume of trade with the United States and other Arab countries in addition to Europe. The role of Egypt's bilateral trading patterns are examined in detail in Konan and Maskus and in Hoekman, Konan, and Maskus.[35] Regional agreements that lead to preferential, rather than MFN, reduction of barriers have a tendency to inefficiently reduce

---

34. Konan and Maskus (2000).
35. Konan and Maskus (2002b); Hoekman, Konan, and Maskus (1998).

the volume of trade with nonmember countries, thus dampening the benefits of liberalization.

A final, less surprising, result of shallow integration is that free trade tends to favor labor in Tunisia and nonproduction labor in Egypt. While the model is one of full employment, this enhanced demand for labor is likely to be reflected in higher employment levels rather than merely higher wages. Finally, the labor and other value added adjustment terms reflect the percentage of the respective factor that would change sector of employment in response to the new policy environment. In Tunisia, about 5.6 percent of the factors would change occupations under a purely preferential agreement and about half that amount would move under an MFN agreement. Note that if a lump-sum tax replacement were used in Tunisia, approximately 7 to 8 percent of factors would be mobile in a shallow integration framework. Factor adjustment costs are much lower in Egypt, with less than 2 percent mobility.

To briefly summarize the lessons learned from this first set of experiments, the liberalization issues confronting Egypt and Tunisia are different in important ways. For Tunisia, a liberalization effort that focuses on trade with Europe will move the economy in a direction very close to that of free trade. The benefit of reducing tariffs is rather substantial. What is dampening Tunisia's ability to benefit from a liberalized trade environment is the distortionary nature of its value-added tax. In the absence of tariff revenues, the VAT becomes a more important tax instrument. Efforts to enhance uniformity of the VAT would complement trade liberalization efforts.

In the case of Egypt, the relatively low volume of trade and openness appears to be due to structural barriers besides simple tariffs. While reforms might be easier to facilitate in the context of an Egypt-EU agreement or a greater Arab initiative, given Egypt's diverse pattern of trade, liberalization that proceeds on a bilateral basis will not be as constructive as multilateral (MFN) efforts. This implies that the path to liberalization is likely to be more complicated for Egypt than for Tunisia.

Deepening Integration among Arab Countries

Table 5-11 considers the possibility of a reduction in tariff and nontariff barriers to trade in goods. As discussed above, nontariff barriers are assumed to arise due to excessive regulatory restrictions, the liberalization of

Table 5-11. *Impact of Deep Reform Scenarios, Tariffs plus Goods Nontariff Barriers*

	GAFTA + Euro-Med agreement (DEM)	Unilateral most favored nation (DAL)	Euro-Med + GAFTA + MFN (DAM)
Tunisia			
Macroeconomic variables (percent change)			
Welfare (EV)	7.71	7.87	7.96
GDP	8.26	8.82	8.85
Consumer price index	−7.16	−7.29	−7.37
Wage	10.44	10.48	10.07
Price of other value added	2.21	2.43	2.76
Value added tax	0.17	0.23	0.24
Labor adjustment	5.51	5.13	4.57
Other value added adjustment	5.66	5.12	4.71
Production (share of GDP)			
Agriculture (19.5%)[a]	15.62	16.30	16.05
Manufacturing (33%)[a]	43.00	41.85	41.82
Mining and utilities (7%)[a]	6.34	5.44	6.43
Services excluding tourism (41%)[a]	35.04	36.40	35.70
Egypt			
Macroeconomic variables (percent change)			
Welfare (EV)	2.74	2.93	3.31
GDP	1.87	1.33	1.49
Consumer price index	−6.15	−6.33	−6.67
Wage production labor	3.88	3.42	4.06
Wage nonproduction labor	4.80	4.99	5.64
Price of other value added	3.56	3.75	3.98
Goods and services tax	−7.47	14.86	15.21
Production labor adjustment	1.88	2.36	2.67
Nonproduction labor adjustment	1.44	1.82	2.05
Other value added adjustment	1.65	2.28	2.37
Production (share of GDP)			
Agriculture (22.6%)[a]	20.45	20.96	20.32
Manufacturing (39.8%)[a]	40.25	39.93	39.52
Mining and utilities (3.7%)[a]	3.47	3.88	3.52
Services excluding tourism (33.4%)[a]	35.84	35.23	36.63

Source: Author's calculations.

a. Benchmark figure.

which would lower trading costs with all trading partners. In addition to the removal of NTBs on a nondiscriminatory basis, three tariff liberalization scenarios are considered. In the first column, tariffs on imports from Arab countries and the EU are eliminated (and reciprocal export market access to those regions improved). Next, tariffs are eliminated with all trading partners. Finally, the benefits of the GAFTA and EU-Mediterranean initiative are combined with unilateral tariff reduction in the third column.

Three clear messages arise out of a liberalization scenario involving the elimination of tariffs and nontariff barriers to trade in goods. One is that the rewards of deep integration are significantly higher than those of traditional shallow integration, especially for Egypt. In the case of Tunisia, percentage welfare gains are more than twice as high, with almost an 8 percent improvement in welfare (EV) and a more than 8 percent expansion in GDP in all cases. Egyptian welfare gains associated with MFN tariff reduction in the context of the Euro-Med initiative and enhanced market access to Arab partners through the GAFTA increase from 0.6 percent when reforms are limited to tariffs to 3.3 percent with deep integration. As discussed above, it may be that Egypt's regulatory and administrative barriers impose higher costs on trade than do those of Tunisia. In a counterfactual scenario in which Egyptian NTBs were assumed to be twice as high as those of Tunisia, deep integration provided an equivalent variation welfare gain ranging from 5 to 6 percent and an increase in GDP of about 3 percent.

Second, the gains from deep integration are rather similar regardless of whether barriers are reduced through unilateral reform or through a regional agreement. This second finding relies on the modeling assumption that administrative barriers are applied on a nondiscriminatory basis. An alternative possibility is that regulatory and administrative barriers can be reduced on a preferential basis. In the case of Egypt, such scenarios for deep integration are considered in Hoekman and Konan.[36]

Third, the adjustment costs of deep integration, in terms of movement of factors, appear to be roughly similar to those of shallow integration, as are the required changes in the endogenous domestic tax instrument. Thus deep integration goes no further than shallow integration in changing

---

36. Hoekman and Konan (2000, 2001).

employment and production patterns and thus is no more costly in terms of restructuring the economy.

Service Sector Liberalization Yields Large Payoffs

Key findings from the Konan and Maskus study of the impact of services liberalization on the Tunisian economy are presented in table 5-12 and compared with results obtained for Egypt.[37] An initial observation is that while the benefits of service liberalization are quite significant, what is required is a reform package that facilitates foreign direct investment. The scope for gains from liberalizing cross-border barriers is limited due to the low volume of services traded across borders. As discussed above, many services require personal interaction between producer and client, impeding the cross-border exchange of services (mode 1 GATS).

If barriers to foreign investment were lowered, the estimated gains would be substantial, with an equivalent variation gain in welfare of 7 percent for Egypt and 8 percent for Tunisia. For Tunisia, these gains are comparable to those estimated to be achievable through deep liberalization of goods trade. The Egyptian economy apparently would more readily benefit from liberalization that focuses on services than on a reform package concerned only with barriers to trade in goods.

In the case of Tunisia, while the gains from liberalizing investment in services are similar to those attainable under deep integration of goods markets, the impacts on the economy are markedly different. Deep integration involves restructuring the economy toward manufacturing and away from other sectors, most notably agriculture and services.[38] In contrast, services liberalization appears to involve rather minimal adjustments in the movement of factors across sectors and in the overall structure of the economy. Liberalization of services in Tunisia benefits nonlabor sources of value added disproportionately, whereas goods liberalization favors workers. Surprisingly, services liberalization in Egypt appears to benefit production labor and other sources of value added, with nonproduction labor (concentrated in the provision of services) apparently benefiting little.

---

37. Konan and Maskus (2001).

38. Egypt's economy appears to be less responsive to deep integration and gains achievable are less pronounced.

Table 5-12. *Impact of Service Sector Liberalization Scenarios*

	Border liberalization (S1)	Investment liberalization (SR3)	Full liberalization (SAL)
Tunisia			
Macroeconomic variables			
(percent change)			
Welfare (EV)	0.95	7.90	9.11
GDP	0.74	7.79	8.78
Consumer price index	−0.94	−7.32	−8.35
Wage	0.37	3.50	4.38
Price of other value added	1.15	8.12	9.28
Labor adjustment	0.81	3.32	3.67
Other value added adjustment	1.02	4.68	5.19
Production (share of GDP)			
Agriculture (19.5%)[a]	19.95	21.08	21.28
Manufacturing (33%)[a]	31.61	29.41	28.83
Mining and utilities (7%)[a]	7.09	6.61	6.62
Services excluding			
tourism (41%)[a]	41.36	42.90	43.28
Egypt			
Macroeconomic variables			
(percent change)			
Welfare (EV)	0.79	6.77	7.31
GDP	2.49	8.39	8.71
Consumer price index	−4.33	−9.69	−10.15
Wage production labor	2.71	8.65	9.08
Wage nonproduction labor	2.25	0.37	0.50
Price of other value added	2.43	7.87	8.40
Production labor adjustment	0.78	2.49	2.47
Nonproduction labor adjustment	0.55	4.52	4.52
Other value added adjustment	0.89	1.19	1.25
Production (share of GDP)			
Agriculture (22.6%)[a]	21.26	21.03	21.02
Manufacturing (39.8%)[a]	41.88	41.77	41.77
Mining and utilities (3.7%)[a]	3.96	3.74	4.11
Services excluding			
tourism (33.4%)[a]	32.89	33.47	33.10

Source: Author's calculations.
a. Benchmark figure.

Concluding Remarks

This section summarizes key insights for Tunisia and Egypt. Selected alternative integration scenarios, most of which already have been discussed, are given in table 5-13.

Overall Implications for Tunisia

In the case of Tunisia, the benefits of liberalizing services trade are somewhat higher than those achievable through eliminating goods barriers (both tariffs and NTBs, column DAM) and significantly higher than the benefits of traditional shallow integration (column SHM). If the category of shallow integration is expanded to include the reduction of barriers to services trade (mode 1) (column SGSM), welfare increases modestly. Column DGSM shows the result of an extensive reform in which goods tariffs and NTBs are eliminated and foreign trade *and* investment in the service sector are liberalized. The potential gains are remarkable—roughly 16 percent in both equivalent variation (welfare) and in output. These gains are somewhat less than the sum of the gains attributed to goods liberalization (DAM) and to services liberalization (SAL) in isolation, implying that the *reforms impact the economy with modest interaction.* As mentioned earlier, the distortionary nature of Tunisia's value-added tax offsets some of the gains to be had from most liberalization scenarios. Due to a low volume of bilateral trade, a simple regional trade arrangement (in absence of the Euro-Mediterranean initiative) would tend to be trade diversionary and to lower welfare and output. On the basis of its economic impact, the decision of Tunisian policymakers to conduct reform efforts in the context of Tunisia's relationship with Europe appears to be rational.

Overall Implications for Egypt

As shown in table 5-13, Egypt would gain only modestly from traditional trade agreements that focus only on tariff barriers (column SHM). The relatively low volume of Egyptian trade appears to be attributable to factors not captured by tariff rates, as previously discussed. For reform to have a major impact on Egypt's economy would require reduction of structural impediments to trade. Two such extensive reforms are considered. In the first, it is assumed that NTBs on goods are reduced in conjunction with the elimination of tariffs and with regional agreements through which barriers

Table 5-13. *Impact of Alternative GAFTA Reform Scenarios*

	Tariffs only		Tariffs + goods NTBs				
	GAFTA (SME)	GAFTA + Euro-Med + MFN (SHM)	GAFTA + Euro-Med (DEM)	GAFTA + Euro-Med + MFN only[a] (DAM)	Service sector liberalization[b] (SAL)	GAFTA + shallow liberalization[b] (SGSM)	GAFTA + deep liberalization[b] (DSGM)
Tunisia							
Macroeconomic variables (percent change)							
Welfare (EV)	−0.07	2.20	7.71	7.96	9.11	2.99	15.97
GDP	−0.02	4.31	8.26	8.85	8.78	4.85	16.49
Consumer price index	0.07	−2.15	−7.16	−7.37	−8.35	−2.90	−13.77
Wage	−0.17	3.41	10.44	10.07	4.38	3.29	10.49
Price of other value added	0.01	0.64	2.21	2.76	9.28	1.89	13.18
Value added tax	0.01	0.29	0.17	0.24	−0.06	0.30	0.21
Labor adjustment	0.15	1.77	5.51	4.57	3.67	1.22	3.31
Other value added adjustment	0.14	2.45	5.66	4.71	5.19	2.38	5.81
Production (share of GDP)							
Agriculture (19.5%)[c]	19.5	18.4	15.6	16.1	21.3	19.1	20.1
Manufacturing (33%)[c]	32.7	36.5	43.0	41.8	28.8	34.5	32.0
Mining and utilities (7%)[c]	7.2	6.1	6.3	6.4	6.6	6.4	6.4
Services excluding tourism (41%)[c]	40.6	39.0	35.0	35.7	43.3	39.9	41.5

Egypt

Macroeconomic variables (percent change)

Welfare (EV)	0.18	0.57	2.74	3.31	7.31	1.14	10.64
GDP	2.05	0.45	1.87	1.49	8.71	0.81	8.20
Consumer price index	−3.75	−4.12	−6.15	−6.67	−10.15	−4.67	−12.85
Wage production labor	2.22	1.82	3.88	4.06	9.08	2.26	11.38
Wage nonproduction labor	2.17	3.21	4.80	5.64	0.50	3.34	4.41
Price of other value added	1.87	2.21	3.56	3.98	8.40	2.78	10.61
Goods and services tax	−43.95	15.52	−7.47	15.21	−76.50	14.79	−16.80
Production labor adjustment	0.45	1.97	1.88	2.67	2.47	1.84	4.89
Nonproduction labor adjustment	0.26	1.57	1.44	2.05	4.52	1.49	5.70
Other value added adjustment	0.53	1.91	1.65	2.37	1.25	1.99	3.25

Production (share of GDP)

Agriculture (22.6%)[c]	21.2	21.1	20.5	20.3	21.0	20.9	20.2
Manufacturing (39.8%)[c]	41.7	40.0	40.3	39.5	41.8	40.2	39.6
Mining and utilities (3.7%)[c]	3.6	3.8	3.5	3.5	4.1	4.3	4.0
Services excluding tourism (33.4%)[c]	33.5	35.1	35.8	36.6	33.1	34.6	36.2

Source: Author's calculations.

a. No change in goods barriers.

b. Liberalization of both goods and services.

c. Benchmark figure.

fall among trading partners (DEM and DAM). The estimates of deep integration effects that follow are comparable to those achievable in Tunisia under simple shallow liberalization scenarios. As it is highly likely that the NTBs reported for Egypt in this chapter underestimate the true extent of the barriers, additional counterfactual experiments were performed in which NTBs to trade in goods were doubled. In that event deep integration would increase welfare by 5 to 6 percent, a significant improvement. It is thus important to gather more evidence on the true impact of Egyptian NTBs. Reform of the service sector, particularly domestically and through foreign investment, appears to offer the most significant prospect for gains.

Appendix 5A. Equations, Variables, and Parameters Used in the Model

Production equations

1. Value added function

$$V_i = [a_{Li}L_i^{(\sigma i-1)/\sigma i} + a_{Ki}K_i^{(\sigma i-1)/\sigma i}]^{\sigma i/(\sigma i-1)}$$

2. Imported intermediates

$$M_{iN} = [\Sigma_r \delta_{ri}m_{riN}^{(\eta i-1)/\eta i}]^{\eta i/(\eta i-1)}$$

3. Composite intermediate

$$z_{ji} = [\gamma_{di}d_{ji}^{(\eta j-1)/\eta j} + \gamma_{mi}m_{ji}^{(\eta j-1)/\eta j}]^{\eta j/(\eta j-1)}$$

4. Final goods technology

$$Y_i = min[z_{1i}/a_{1i}, \ldots, z_{ni}/a_{ni}, V_i/a_{VA}]$$

5. Domestic and foreign sales

$$Y_i = [\alpha_{Di}D_i^{(\epsilon i-1)/\epsilon i} + \alpha_{Xi}X_i^{(\epsilon i-1)/\epsilon i}]^{\epsilon j/(\epsilon j-1)}$$

6. Export allocation

$$X_i = [\Sigma_r \beta_{ri}X_{ri}^{(ei-1)/ei}]^{ei/(ei-1)}$$

7. Marginal cost condition

$$(1+\lambda_i)c_iY_i = \Sigma_j(1+v_j)p_jd_{ji} + \\ \Sigma_j\Sigma_r(1 + u_j + t_{rj})p_{rj}^m m_{rji} + \\ (1 + \tau_{Vi})(w_KK_i + w_LL_{1i})$$

Utility equations

8. Utility function

$$U = \Pi_i C_i^{bi}; \Sigma_i b_i = 1$$

9. Domestic and import consumption (applies also to G_i and I_i^F)

$$C_i = [\phi_{Di}D_{iC}^{(\psi i-1)/\psi i} + \\ \phi_{MiC}M_{iC}^{(\psi i-1)/\psi i}]^{\psi i/(\psi i-1)}$$

10. Import allocation (applies also to M_{iG} and M_{il}^F)

$$M_{iC} = [\Sigma_r \delta_{ri}M_{ric}^{(\eta i-1)/\eta i}]^{\eta i/(\eta i-1)}$$

Equations for constraints and balancing items

11. Agent's budget constraint

$$\Sigma_i \tilde{p}_i^c Ci\, C_i = w_K \bar{E}_K + w_L \Sigma_i L_i + -\Sigma_i \tilde{p}_i^{IF} I_i^F$$
$$-\Sigma_i p_i I_i^I - r^F K^F -$$
$$D + \Sigma_i\, v_i Y_i$$

12. Government budget constraint

$$\Sigma_i \tilde{p}_i G_i = D + \Sigma_i \tau_{Vi} \tilde{p}_i^{\,C} V_i +$$
$$\Sigma_i \Sigma_r (\tau_{Vi} + t_{ri}) p_{ri}^{\,m} (M_{riC} + M_{riI}^{\,F})$$

13. Current account balance

$$0 = \Sigma_r \Sigma_i (1/e)(p_{ri}^{\,m} M_{ri} - p_{ri}^{\,x} X_{ri} -$$
$$w_L^F L^F + r^F K^F)$$

14. Product market clearance

$$S_i = \Sigma_j a_{ij} Y_j + G_i + I_i^F + I_i^I + C_i$$

15. Factor market clearance

$$\Sigma_i K_i = \bar{E}_K\, ; \Sigma_i L_i = \bar{E}_{1L}$$

16. Zero profits

$$p_i\, D_i + \Sigma_r p_{ri}^{\,x} X_{ri} = c_i Y_i$$

17. Supply Value Balance

$$\tilde{p}_i\, S_i = \tilde{p}_i^{\,Z} \Sigma_j a_{ij} (1 + v_i) Y_j + \tilde{p}_i^{\,C} D_{iC} +$$
$$\tilde{p}_i^{\,IF} D_{iI}^{\,F} + \tilde{p}_i^{\,G} D_{iG} + \tilde{p}_i^{\,IF} I_i^I +$$
$$\Sigma_r (1 + \tau_{Vi} + u_i + t_{ri}) p_{ri}^{\,m} (M_{riC} +$$
$$M_{riG} + M_{riI}^{\,F})$$

Price Relationships and Identities

18. Components of domestic sales

$$D_i = D_{iC} + D_{iI}^{\,F} + I_i^I + D_{iG}$$

19. Components of import sales

$$M_i = M_{iN} + M_{iC} + M_{iI}^{\,F} + M_{iG}$$

20. Domestic price of intermediate imports (holds also for imports for G)

$$p_{ri}^{\,N} = (1 + \tau_{Vi} + u_i + t_{ri}) p_{ri}^{\,m}$$

21. Domestic price of imports for C (holds also for imports for I^F)

$$p_{ri}^{\,C} = (1 + \tau_{Vi} + u_i + t_{ri}) p_{ri}^{\,m}$$

22. Consumer price of domestic goods (holds also for purchases for I^F)

$$p_i^{\,C} = (1 + v_i) p_i$$

23. Capital market equilibrium

$$\tau_{K1} + w_{K1} = \ldots = \tau_{Kn} + w_{Kn}$$

Variables

L_i	Domestic labor inputs, sector i $(i = 1, \ldots, 34)$
K_i	Capital (other value added) inputs, both mobile and immobile
V_i	Value added
M_i	Total imports
M_{ri}	Imports from region r $(r = \text{EU, Arab countries, ROW})$
M_{iN}	Imports of commodity i for intermediate use
m_{riN}	Imports for intermediate use from region r $(r = \text{EU, Arab countries, ROW})$
z_{ji}	Composite intermediate input of j into i $(j = 1, \ldots, 34)$
d_{ji}, m_{ji}	Intermediate usages of domestic and imported goods
Y_i	Output of good i
D_i, X_i	Output for domestic sales and exports
$D_{iC}, D_{iG}, D_{iI}{}^F$	Domestic sales: private and public consumption, capital formation
X_{ri}	Exports of good i to region r
c_i	Index of marginal cost of production
p_i	Domestic producer price index
$\tilde{p}_i^Z, \tilde{p}_i^C, \tilde{p}_i^{IF}, \tilde{p}_i^G$	Domestic price indexes (home and imported prices)
w_K, w_L	Factor price indexes
U	Utility
$\tilde{p}_i$	Composite price index for total domestic supply
C_i, G_i	Private and public consumption
I_i^F, I_i^I	Fixed capital formation and inventory investment
M_{iC}, M_{iG}	Imports for private and public consumption
$M_{iI}{}^F$	Imports for fixed capital formation
M_{riC}, M_{riG}	Imports for private and public consumption from region r
$M_{riI}{}^F$	Imports for fixed capital formation from region r
K^F	Net payments on foreign capital holdings
e	Real exchange rate (price index for foreign exchange)
B	Current-account balance
D	Government budget deficit (held fixed)
S_i	Supply on domestic market $(D_i + M_i)$
$p_{ri}{}^N$	Domestic price index for intermediate imports

$p_{ri}^{\,C}, p_{ri}^{\,G}$	Domestic price indexes for imports of private and public consumption
$p_{ril}^{\,F}$	Domestic price index for imports for gross capital formation
$p_i^{\,C}, p_{il}^{\,F}$	Price index for private consumption/fixed capital of domestic goods
p_{ri}	Producer price index for goods exported to region r
τ_{Vi}	Endogenous tax rate on value added

Parameters

σ_i	Substitution elasticity between capital and labor
η_a	Substitution elasticity between intermediates and value added
η_i	Armington elasticity on imports between regions
η_j	Substitution elasticity between domestic and imported intermediates
ϵ_i	Transformation elasticity between domestic and exported output
e_i	Transformation elasticity on exports between regions
ψ_i	Substitution elasticity between domestic and imported consumption
t_{ri}	Tariff rate on imports from region r ($t_{ri} = 0$ for service sectors)
u_i	Resource-using services border barriers ($u_i = 0$ for nonservice sectors)
v_i	Service rents on output ($v_i = 0$ for nonservice sectors)
λ_i	Service resource-using barriers on output ($\lambda_i = 0$ for nonservice sectors)
$\bar{E}_K, \bar{E}_{1L},$	Endowment of capital and labor
$p_{ri}^{\,m}$	Price of imports from region r
$p_{ri}^{\,x}$	Price of exports in region r
r^F	Price of foreign capital payments

References

De Melo, Jaime, and Sherman Robinson. 1989. "Product Differentiation and the Treatment of Foreign Trade in Computable General Equilibrium Models of Small Economies." *Journal of International Economics* 27: 47–67.

Galal, Ahmed. 2000. "Incentives for Economic Integration in the Middle East." In *Trade Policy Developments in the Middle East and North Africa*, edited by Bernard Hoekman and Hanaa Kheir-El-Din. Washington: World Bank.

Galal, Ahmed, and Bernard Hoekman. 1997. *Regional Partners in Global Markets: Limits and Possibilities of the Euro-Mediterranean Agreements*. London: Center for Economic Policy Research.

Galal, Ahmed, and Robert Z. Lawrence, eds. 1998. *Building Bridges: An Egypt-U.S. Free Trade Agreement*. Brookings.

Goaied, Mohamed. 1999. "Cost-Frontier Analysis of Tunisian Commercial Banking Sectors." University of Tunis.

Harrison, Glenn W., and others. 1993. "How Robust Is Applied General Equilibrium Modeling?" *Journal of Policy Modeling* 15: 99–115.

Hoekman, Bernard, and Denise Eby Konan. 2000. "Rents, Red Tape, and Regionalism." In *Catching Up with the Competition: Trade Opportunities and Challenges for Arab Countries*, edited by Bernard Hoekman and Jamel Zarrouk. University of Michigan Press.

———. 2001. "Deep Integration, Non-Discrimination, and Euro-Mediterranean Free Trade." In *Regionalism in Europe: Geometries and Strategies After 2000*, edited by Jürgen von Hagen and Mika Widgren. Boston: Kluwer Academic Publishers.

Hoekman, Bernard, Denise Eby Konan, and Keith E. Maskus. 1998. "An Egypt-U.S. Free Trade Agreement: Economic Incentives and Effects." In *Building Bridges: An Egypt-U.S. Free Trade Agreement*, edited by Ahmed Galal and Robert Lawrence. Brookings.

Institute National de la Statistique. 1998. *Les Comptes de la Nation Base 1983: Agregats et Tableaux d'Ensemble, 1993–1997*. Tunis: INS Press.

International Monetary Fund. 2000. *IMF Balance of Payments Statistical Yearbook*. Washington.

Kalirajan, Kaleeswaran, and others. 2000. "The Price Impact of Restrictions on Banking Services." Mimeo. Australian Productivity Commission.

Kheir-El-Din, Hanaa. 2000. "Enforcement of Product Standards as Barriers to Trade: The Case of Egypt." In *Trade Policy Developments in the Middle East and North Africa*, edited by Bernard Hoekman and Hanaa Kheir-El-Din. Washington: World Bank.

Konan, Denise Eby, and Keith E. Maskus. 1997. "A Computable General Equilibrium Analysis of Egyptian Trade Liberalization Scenarios." In *Regional Partners in Global Markets*.

————. 2000. "Joint Trade Liberalization and Tax Reform in a Small Open Economy: The Case of Egypt." *Journal of Development Economics* 61: 365–92.

————. 2002a. "Quantifying Services Liberalization in a Developing Economy." World Bank Working Paper. Washington: World Bank.

————. 2002b. "Bilateral Trade Patterns and Welfare: An Egypt-EU Preferential Trade Agreement." In *New Development of International Trade: Theoretical and Empirical Investigation*, edited by S. Katayama. REIB Kobe University.

Lawrence, Robert Z. 1996. *Regionalism, Multilateralism, and Deeper Integration.* Brookings.

Maskus, Keith E., and Denise Eby Konan. 1997. "Trade Liberalization in Egypt." *Review of Development Economics* 1 (3): 275–93.

Nabli, Mustapha K., and Annette I. De Kleine. 2000. "Managing Global Integration in the Middle East and North Africa." In *Trade Policy Developments in the Middle East and North Africa*.

Rutherford, T., E. E. Rutstrom, and David Tarr. 2000. "A Free Trade Agreement between the European Union and a Representative Arab Mediterranean Country." In *Catching Up with the Competition: Trade Opportunities and Challenges for Arab Countries*, edited by Bernard Hoekman and Jamel Zarrouk. University of Michigan Press.

World Bank. 2000. *Tunisia: Social and Structural Review 2000: Integrating into the World Economy and Sustaining Economic and Social Progress.* Washington.

Zarrouk, Jamel. 2000a. "Regulatory Regimes and Trade Costs." In *Catching Up with the Competition.*

————. 2000b. "Para-Tariff Measures in Arab Countries." In *Trade Policy Developments in the Middle East and North Africa.*

————. 2000c. "The Greater Arab Free Trade Area: Limits and Possibilities." In *Catching Up with the Competition.*

————. 2001. "A Survey of Barriers to Trade and Investment in the MENA Region." Report prepared for the Council on Foreign Relations (New York).

6

Initial Conditions and Incentives for Arab Economic Integration: Can the European Community's Success Be Emulated?

BERNARD HOEKMAN
PATRICK MESSERLIN

R egional integration is a central element of the trade strategies being pursued by many Arab countries. All countries in the region have concluded numerous bilateral agreements to reduce trade barriers on a preferential basis, and many members of the Arab League are engaged in an effort to abolish tariffs on intra-Arab trade flows altogether. Most Arab countries around the Mediterranean also have signed free trade agreements with the European Community (EC) that aim at eliminating tariffs on trade in goods (with the exception of agricultural products) and that also embody elements of "deeper" integration—provisions calling for cooperation in trade-related regulatory areas and future negotiation to liberalize the flow of investment and services.

The authors thank Mustapha Nabli, Mounir Abdel Nour, Ahmed Galal, Heba Handoussa, Denise Konan, and Maurice Schiff for helpful comments and Francis Ng for assistance with the data. This chapter draws in part on the results of a Council on Foreign Relations study group on trade policy options for the Middle East and North Africa summarized in Hoekman and Messerlin (2002). The views expressed do not necessarily reflect those of the World Bank or its board of executive directors and the governments they represent.

While efforts to liberalize trade between Arab countries on a preferential basis have been limited in scope, the implementation of the 1998 Greater Arab Free Trade Agreement (GAFTA), which obliges signatories to gradually eliminate tariffs by 2008, is beginning to change that.[1] However, GAFTA is a traditional agreement that is limited to merchandise trade; in contrast to the EC treaty, it does not imply the creation of a common market for services, investment, and other factor flows. Nor does it involve the establishment of common institutions to address regulatory issues.

This chapter seeks to identify what those pursuing Arab integration can learn from the European integration experience. It does not address the issue of whether there is (or will be) political support for greater economic integration—it investigates instead what incentives Arab countries have to pursue alternative forms of regional economic cooperation. The initial conditions that prevailed in the EC are identified, and a description is offered of how member states dealt with major political obstacles to integration through the design of the EC's institutions. EC trade fundamentals then are compared to those that apply in the current Arab context. The results show that the fundamentals differ significantly, suggesting that Arab integration will have to follow a path that goes beyond an approach based solely on the liberalization of trade in merchandise.

One alternative path identified is an integration strategy driven by the service sector. Given the importance of improving service sector performance in many Arab countries and the potential gains from regional cooperation in the regulatory domain, such a strategy may be a more effective route toward greater integration, not just among countries in the region—where there is only limited potential and therefore probably limited political support—but into the world economy. The EC experience suggests that a services-based integration strategy will be complex and should be carefully designed and sequenced. Intra-Arab cooperation in this area could start by focusing on addressing high logistics- and trade-related transaction costs (trade facilitation); establishing focal points and benchmarks for regulation of key "backbone" services such as transport, distribution, and communications; and making a concerted effort to remove entry barriers and government restrictions on competition in general.

1. Zarrouk (2000).

Key Dimensions of the European Community

The basic principle guiding the formation of modern Europe has been to use an economic process to achieve a fundamentally political goal: the "ever closer union of the peoples of Europe."[2] It is important to understand that this goal was based on a number of historical and economic factors.[3] For example, in the nineteenth century Europe had been integrated through force of arms by Napoleon, which led to significant convergence in legislation and administrative procedures. Also relevant was how numerous German states combined through the mechanism of the Zollverein into a federal Germany. However, more recent historical events played the primary role in the formation of the EC, in particular World War II. The desire to prevent war was an overriding objective of many of those who supported European integration in the 1950s, based on their strong perception of a positive correlation between trade and peace.[4]

Before the Second World War European countries relied heavily on trade with each other. The collapse of trade in the 1930s and 1940s provided a strong incentive to remove the barriers that had been built up before and during the war. The challenge was to satisfy the political need to maintain critical national industries and the support of powerful interest groups while allowing for greater gains from trade to be captured. As is well known, the interwar years were characterized by large-scale intervention in trade and beggar-thy-neighbor competitive devaluations. The objective of integrating Europe provided a mechanism for reopening European markets.

An important feature of the EC is the success that it has had in managing the trade-off between *net* economic costs and political benefits for members. Europeans eager to create some kind of federal Europe were ready to adopt policies that were more interventionist and costly from an economic efficiency point of view than Europeans interested "merely" in peaceful coexistence between European states. The search for balance between economic and political goals has played a major role in the European

2. Treaty of Rome, preamble, first paragraph.
3. What follows draws in part on Messerlin (2001). See Milward (1992) for a historical analysis of European economic integration.
4. Mansfield (1994) has concluded that, controlling for other factors, there is a robust negative relationship between the volume of trade between country pairs and the probability of a war between them.

Community's history. Political objectives were critical in the development of the EC, in the sense that decisions that were costly from an economic perspective were possible because of associated political gains. As a consequence, any perceptions that the political gains from European integration are decreasing require a reduction in the economic costs to maintain the balance. Political gains from integration are subject to diminishing returns. The political idea of a perpetual peace between France and Germany had a profound appeal to Europeans born before the 1960s; however, in 2002, the idea of a Franco-German war is so remote that younger Europeans see no need to pay the economic costs that previous generations of Europeans were ready to pay. Such shifting balances have led to efforts by the EC to expand membership and deepen integration, and they help explain why external protection has fallen over time.

Institutions

The basic constituent elements of the EC are well known. A major objective of the Treaty of Rome, which established the European Economic Community, was the realization of the four freedoms: free internal movement of goods, services, labor, and capital, including the right of establishment. Thus the EC aims to establish a common market with a common external commercial policy. The community is unique in that it goes beyond intergovernmental cooperation. That is reflected, inter alia, in the fact that EC law has direct effect and that the EC has supranational institutions: an executive body (the European Commission), a political oversight body (the European Council), a judiciary (the European Court of Justice), and a directly elected European Parliament. Of these, the European Commission and the European Court of Justice (ECJ) have been most important in the pursuit of political and economic integration.

The supranational institutions of the EC have played a major role in the process of integration. The European Commission has been the driver and guardian of integration. It has the power to propose directives and regulations, which, if approved by the council and increasingly by the parliament, become EC law. Because those laws have direct effect, they supersede national legislation in the area concerned. The commission is a bureaucracy, staffed by nationals of the EC who are formally independent of their governments. The European Council—comprising the relevant ministers of member states or their heads of state, depending on the subject matter under consideration—provides national-level political oversight. The council must approve all commission proposals, working on either the basis of unanimity or weighted voting, again depending on the topic. Over time, an increasing number of issues have become subject to voting.

The European Commission administers the common policies of the EC, including trade and agriculture policy—the two most important areas.[5] It also enforces the various treaties that have been concluded or amended over time. Of great importance here is enforcement of rules on "fair" competition, such as those regarding state aid (subsidies) and restrictive business practices by firms, which have the effect of impeding trade and the realization of an integrated internal market. The commission has an interest in both expanding its ambit—through promulgation of new rules in the pursuit of integration—and enforcing the negotiated rules of the game. The commission, an independent *European* bureaucracy with its own financing—partly obtained from the revenues generated by the common external tariff—has defended the European integration objective when member states have been less than enthusiastic.[6] The commission played a major role, for example, in forming a coalition with the private sector in the 1980s to revitalize integration through the Single Market Program. This proved to be a powerful instrument for furthering the objective of economic integration by introducing the principle of mutual recognition and "competition in rules" and by taking a series of concrete measures to enhance competition in services markets. This resulted in a boom in foreign direct investment inflows and cross-border mergers and acquisitions and induced the accession of a number of countries that had concluded that the costs of being outside the EC had become greater than the benefits.

The European Commission plays a major role in administering various mechanisms that redistribute income and resources across groups in the EC. Any liberalization of trade gives rise to losers, who, depending on their political power, may need to be compensated. Indeed, if the losers are powerful, compensation is a precondition of liberalization, unless there are

5. The Treaty of Rome grants the European Community (not the European Commission, but a complex mix of the Council of Ministers and the commission) *exclusive* competence in trade policy. However, the way the treaty defines the scope of this common and exclusive competence is rather clumsy. Article 133 (113 in the initial Treaty of Rome) provides only a nonexhaustive list of trade policy instruments. As a result, determining what is and what is not covered required decades of rulings by the ECJ.

6. Winters, chapter 7 of this volume.

other groups in society whose gains would be sufficient to induce them to mobilize against those who benefit from existing trade restrictions. The compensation required to make trade reform politically feasible can take the form of an exception to trade liberalization, long transition periods, transfers from the budget (subsidies), or linkage to other issues of concern to interest groups. All of these mechanisms were used in the EC. The common policies on trade and agriculture were carefully designed to maintain relatively higher rates of protection for sensitive industries, complemented by transfers (subsidies) to disadvantaged regions and soft lending by the European Investment Bank for infrastructure and related types of projects.

The second major player in the integration venture has been the ECJ, which over time has developed a huge case law literature interpreting the legality of national policies. The decisions of the ECJ, the ultimate arbiter, are final and binding on member states. The court played a key role in the design of the Single Market Program by identifying the significant scope that existed for the principle of mutual recognition to overcome national nontrade policies that impeded cross-border competition. More generally, it has ensured objective and consistent application and interpretation of EC law.

Trade and Trade Policy

The first milestone in the realization of the common market was the creation of a customs union—that is, the adoption of a common external tariff (CET) and the liberalization of internal trade. To a very large extent, trade and trade policy held the EC together.

—*Trade*. In the mid-1950s, each of the six founding EC member states exported more than 25 percent of their total exports to the rest of the community. Thus, all the founding members had both a substantial stake in intra-European liberalization of trade and enough power to have a voice in the creation of the EC. Germany, the largest member, exported almost 30 percent of its total exports to the rest of the EC, accounting for one-third of total intra-EC trade. This "initial condition" is of great importance in understanding the success of the EC: members had not only great political interest in cementing a binding peace but also great economic interest in revitalizing and further expanding intra-European trade. Note that the trade involved merchandise. Trade in services, labor, and capital was quite limited.

—*Trade policy*. Agreeing on a CET and applying it has been among the most difficult aspects of implementing customs unions, as illustrated by the Gulf Cooperation Council, as well as many other attempts to form a customs union.[7] The more unbalanced the initial tariffs across prospective members, the harder the task, unless high-protection countries are seeking to use the customs union as an instrument to liberalize trade. Sustaining the CET can be equally if not more difficult. Any common tariff will imply adjustment pressure as industries relocate, and industry interests will diverge across countries. In the nineteenth century, for example, the American South objected strenuously to the high protective tariffs sought by U.S. "infant" industries, which were located mostly in the North. The tariffs raised production costs in the South and implied a transfer of resources to the North, exacerbating the tensions that led to the U.S. Civil War. Similar tensions associated with industrial agglomeration and implicit transfers helped the demise of the East African Common Market.[8] The initial conditions confronting EC members regarding the formation of the CET were relatively favorable. The EC created its common tariff from four initial tariff schedules (Belgium, the Netherlands, and Luxembourg already were a single customs territory, the Benelux, with a common tariff schedule). Two territories (Germany and Benelux) had rather low tariffs, and two (France and Italy) had relatively high tariffs—an ideal circumstance for using the simplest possible harmonization rule: apply the unweighted average of the four tariff schedules. This greatly facilitated agreement on the level of the external tariff, limiting disputes between EC member states to tariff lines where duty rates were different enough to make everybody unsatisfied by the outcome of the unweighted average method. The number of such cases—about 20 percent of all tariff lines—was not negligible.[9] The General Agreement on Tarrifs and Trade (GATT) helped resolve many of these conflicts by lowering tariffs across the board through multilateral negotiating rounds—making the results of the averaging method more palatable to the more open member states while offering compensation to more protectionist members by giving them better access to global export markets.

Liberalization of internal trade was accompanied by managed trade in key sectors such as the coal, steel, and agriculture industries as well as by the

7. World Bank, *World Development Indicators*, 2001.
8. World Bank, *World Development Indicators*, 2001.
9. Messerlin (2001).

implementation of a common external trade policy. The latter played a major role in the EC, becoming to some extent a substitute for foreign policy. The absence of other means for the EC to take international action—there being no common foreign policy—induced it to carve out zones of political influence through the intensive use of discriminatory trade agreements. These agreements have had almost no economic impact on the EC. Rather, their role has been to establish or strengthen the hegemony of certain EC member states. The primary example of this over the past forty years is the role that EC trade policy has played in supporting the "territorial expansion" of the EC, which grew from the six founding members in 1957 to nine members in 1973, ten in 1981, twelve in 1986, and fifteen in 1995 (leaving aside East Germany in 1990, whose inclusion had been prepared for since the EC's inception and was confirmed by special trade arrangements between the German Democratic Republic and the EC starting in the 1960s).

Common Sectoral Policies

European integration has been driven in part by two sectoral engines: the agriculture industry and the coal and steel industries. The EC has a common policy in both areas, and in both the focus of the common policy is on managing production and trade. In the case of coal and steel, the 1951 Treaty of Paris establishing the European Coal and Steel Community (ECSC), the precursor of the EC, reflected a strong tradition of collusion between steel firms backed by national governments.[10] In the early 1950s, intra-EC free trade in steel was impossible given German comparative advantages, and substituting prevailing private barriers for public management and control therefore made a lot of political sense. But the price paid was the inhibition and distortion of competition in the industry for the next five decades. Perhaps equally if not more important, it also provided a demonstration effect for other sectors, which were given an incentive to push for and support industrial policies that benefited them.

Although the coal and steel industries were of fundamental importance in the design and launch of the European integration effort—not least

10. The ECSC provisions were influenced by the Entente Internationale de l'Acier (International Steel Cartel), set up in 1926 by steel makers from Belgium, France, Germany, Saarland, and Luxembourg. The entente reflected the prevailing view that cartels were a good mechanism for ensuring market stability in the context of intra-European trade liberalization.

because they were seen as a major potential source of conflict between France and Germany—agriculture was equally important. In all six founding member states in the early 1950s, farming claimed a significant share of the labor force and of GDP. Managed trade in this sector was seen as a necessary condition to pursuing integration more broadly. The common agricultural policy (CAP) aimed to increase farm productivity, ensure a fair standard of living for the agricultural community, stabilize markets, and ensure the availability of supplies at reasonable prices. Until the early 1990s, the CAP was essentially based on using *one* instrument (price supports) to reach *all* of those objectives, causing steadily increasing distortions and costs. The political rationale for the CAP—as in the case of coal and steel— was that free trade, even in principle, was neither feasible nor desirable. As far as the two major players were concerned, Germany wanted access to the large French market, which was highly protected—as were almost all EC markets—but could be bought off by the promise of higher prices for agricultural produce.[11]

Over time, virtually all agricultural goods became subject to common market organizations (CMOs). Until the 1992 CAP reform, the CMOs relied essentially on a set of multiple guaranteed prices determined on an annual or biannual basis by the Council of Ministers. Because these guaranteed prices were unrelated to world prices, the CAP required import barriers to insulate the product markets concerned from the world market. Those barriers took the form of variable import levies. Adjusted on a daily basis, the levies raised import prices to the level prevailing in the EC. In the 1970s, export subsidies became necessary in order to dump surpluses into world markets. As of the 1980s, the CAP imposed such a budgetary burden on the EC that quantitative limits on production were imposed, voluntary set-aside programs were adopted, and subsidies were granted to low-income consumers to increase demand.

The CAP was a great success in terms of expanding output and increasing self-sufficiency in food. Indeed, it was too successful—creating serious budgetary strains and, more important for the rest of the world, imposing major costs on non-European food producers and generating decades of multilateral tension. Although the raison d'etre for the CAP has largely disappeared, agricultural reform remains highly contentious in the EC. Sup-

---

11. Winters, chapter 7 of this volume.

port for agricultural and related rural policies to support farmers remains strong, although increasingly they are driven by environmental and public health concerns—which ironically are due in part to the production-increasing incentives of the CAP.

Domestic Regulation

It has been argued that Europe could not make much progress toward trade liberalization until "it was discovered . . . that further progress depended on . . . some policy of 'positive' integration . . . because the removal of discriminatory policies threatened to undermine just as many entrenched interests as [policy integration] would have done."[12] The rhetoric of EC policymakers and their advisers suggested that deeper integration—extending to domestic regulatory regimes and economic policies—was necessary to attain intra-EC free trade. Policymakers such as Jelle Zijlstra, the Dutch minister of economic affairs, were not alone in arguing in the early 1950s that credible tariff removal required "common policies on taxes, wages, prices and employment policy."[13] Many felt that policy harmonization was required to equalize costs and that without it a customs union would not be feasible, because countries would impose new forms of protectionist policies. Thus, the Belgian coal mining industry argued in the late 1940s that a common market could be accepted only if German wage and social security costs were raised to Belgian levels.[14] French officials persistently demanded policy harmonization in the social area—equal pay for both sexes, a uniform length of the working week—as a precondition for trade liberalization, given that French standards were higher than those in other countries.

Underlying these concerns was the general fear among interest groups of an erosion of rents or the worry that domestic policies would be used to reimpose protection. Abstracting from the common policies for the coal and steel and agriculture sectors—where managed trade and production were seen as desirable and necessary—the EC established disciplines in a number of policy areas on the ability of governments to use domestic policy instruments as

12. Milward (1984, p. 421).
13. Milward (1992, pp. 188ff).
14. In the discussion of proposals for a European customs union in the early 1950s, virtually every question that came to be addressed in the Maastricht treaty was raised: a common European currency, monetary policy, whether there should be freedom of labor, mutual recognition of professional qualifications, a common company law, a free capital market, and common workplace and product safety standards (Milward 1992, p. 191).

a substitute for trade policy. Disciplines on enterprise behavior that impeded the realization of the common market and on government assistance—subsidies—were enforced by the European Commission with varying degrees of intensity, but they had an important effect in ensuring that the "conditions of competition" became more equitable over time.

A noteworthy feature of the EC has been the actions it has taken toward deeper integration by harmonizing national policies dealing with regulatory objectives. Those actions have focused on limiting the market-segmenting effects of national regulations pertaining to health and safety. Progress toward harmonization was very slow, in part because adoption of an EC-wide norm required unanimity. It took fourteen years for agreement to be reached on the composition of fruit jams; eleven for a directive on mineral water.[15] Over the 1962–79 period only nine directives on foodstuffs were adopted.

In 1979, the ECJ threw out a German ban on the sale of a French product, Cassis de Dijon, used to prepare the aperitif kir because the ban could not be justified on the basis of public health or safety. In so doing, the ECJ established the principle that goods legally introduced into circulation in one member state could not be barred from entering and being sold in another. This principle was later incorporated into the 1987 Single European Act and the 1992 Maastricht Treaty on European Union. The "new" approach differentiates between standards that have health and safety (public interest) dimensions from those that do not. For the latter it made harmonization redundant by requiring governments to accept foreign regulations as equivalent to their own. For the former a process of determining common minimum standards ("essential requirements") was agreed to. Progress toward development of these standards was made easier by a decision to accept qualified majority voting on issues affecting the functioning and completion of the single market and by defining standardization as a Single Market Program issue.

In sum, integration in the EC was driven very much by the engine of trade in goods—all members had strong incentives to see intra-EC trade liberalized. Trade in services and factors of production—labor, capital—played only a minor role. The EC's success was based in part on an almost perfect balance of economic power. It was "financed" by three large coun-

15. Vogel (1995).

tries—France, Germany, and Italy—of almost equal size in terms of population and income and by two smaller countries—Belgium and the Netherlands—that were large and skilled enough to play the key role of mediator. The EC founding countries, which traded more than 30 percent of their total external trade with the other members, had almost perfectly symmetrical and large stakes in the EC endeavor. Their mutual trade dependence and relative symmetry allowed the EC to use trade liberalization as a vehicle for integration—there was no need to rely significantly on integration of services or labor markets to achieve the members' goals.

This balance was maintained in the enlargement process—the initial balances were never seriously called into question. Britain was as powerful as France or Germany, and Spain was comparable to Italy. Other new members were similar in size to the smaller founding countries. A retrospective sense of the "luck" that accompanied the birth and development of the EC during its first fifty years is best provided by the sudden, but short-lived, hesitations in Europe that accompanied German reunification. Britain and France immediately reacted with their old instinctive fears, while other member states also demonstrated concern. These reactions suggest that the EC probably would not have been founded if Germany had been unified at the time.

Integration also had an overriding political objective that was strongly supported by all members—preventing another war in Europe. The EC is the child of three terrible wars (in 1870, 1914, and 1939) that were responsible for the deaths of millions in the six EC founding countries. It was born in a world divided into two political and economic camps: market-driven democracies and centrally planned dictatorships. During its first thirty years, it grew under the constant pressure of the cold war.

To what extent do the economic factors—in particular the initial trade dependence conditions—that prevailed in the EC apply to the Arab context? As the motor of European integration was to a very large extent the liberalization of intraregional trade in nonagricultural merchandise, an obvious question is whether such trade could also be the basis of Arab economic integration.

Merchandise Trade Fundamentals in Arab Countries

Countries in the Arab region can be divided fairly naturally into three groups: countries that are relatively poor in natural resources (natural resources constitute less than one-third of exports); oil exporters (more than two-thirds of exports consist of natural resources—mostly fuels); and an intermediate group whose exports of fuels and ores constitute between one- and two-thirds of total exports. For completeness and purposes of comparison we report data for other countries in the region—Cyprus, Israel, Turkey, and Iran—as well as for Arab states.

National and Regional Small Product Markets

The *economic* size of the Arab region is limited. Total GDP of Arab countries that are members of the Greater Arab Free Trade Area (noted with an asterisk in table 6-1) represents a little less than Spain's GDP. Only one Arab country, Egypt, has more than 60 million inhabitants. One implication of the "smallness" of many of the countries in the region is that the costs to trade and investment due to differences in national laws or regulations are higher than those for the EC. (Four EC states have a population of more than 60 million, and only two of the fifteen states have a population of less than 5 million.) The limited market size of the Arab countries is a crucial factor in explaining why all efforts to achieve regional economic integration since the 1950s have failed—even if one leaves aside the fact that they were conceived behind high protection with respect to the rest of the world.

There is another powerful economic force working against integration: Arab countries are relatively similar to each other and compete more with each other for the same export markets. Most Arab countries in the sample are either oil-rich or rely heavily on oil exports. As the fundamental motive for trade is to take advantage of differences in the endowments (comparative advantage) of trading partners, their similarity suggests limited prospects for large benefits from regional economic integration. Offsetting this is the fact that Arab countries exhibit a wide range of GDP per capita, from less than US$500 (Yemen) to US$17,000 (UAE and Qatar). Such large income differences generate incentives to trade by inducing product differentiation in order to respond to different incomes and related tastes. But the differences appear too wide for the small markets involved to be a powerful force for significantly greater intraregional trade. That leaves the possibility of a production sharing or processing type of trade through which labor, energy, or water-intensive parts of the production process are undertaken in countries where such factors are in relative abundance. This type of trade has become important in Central Europe, North America, and East Asia. However, for this to materialize there must be a substantial increase in the efficiency of services (a reduction in transaction costs).

In sum, the data suggest that the region is fragmented into relatively small economies that taken together constitute a bloc that is relatively small in economic size; that many have similar production structures, which limits their incentives to trade; and that the wide income differences in the region are unlikely to overcome the resulting trade resistance.

Product Concentration and Differentiation

As natural resources dominate the exports of a majority of Arab countries, we have focused so far on "interindustry" trade, which is based on specialization in production, with countries producing different products using different factor intensities. Such trade may be associated with a concentrated export structure if the country's comparative advantage in a limited range of products is very strong. Interindustry trade is complemented by "intra-industry" trade, which involves the exchange of different varieties of similar "products" or the exchange of goods that form part of a production chain (importing components and exporting the processed goods). In most high-income and newly industrializing countries, intra-industry trade accounts for a large and growing share of total trade.

The scope for intra-industry trade is more limited for fuels than for consumer electronics, but it exists even within the oil sector, broadly defined. There are many varieties of fuels and numerous possibilities to produce differentiated oil-based industrial products, such as chemicals. The potential for specialization and intra-industry trade is augmented by the fact that oil and chemical markets are oligopolistic enough to induce the few large firms operating in such markets to follow a policy of profit maximization through market segmentation and product differentiation. More generally, intra-industry trade is driven by economies of scale that make it profitable for enterprises to specialize in and exchange similar but differentiated goods.

Various measures of the structure and composition of trade are reported in table 6-2. Two indicators of product concentration in trade are reported: the number of distinct product categories exported, measured at the three-digit level of the Standard International Trade Classification

Table 6-1. Overview of Trade Aspects of Middle East and North African Economies, 1998

Countries[a]	WTO status	Population (millions)	GDP (US$ millions)[b]	GDP per capita (US$)[b]	Goods and services[c] (US$ millions)[b] Exports	Imports	Trade openness ratio[d] (percent)	Percent of natural resources in total exports All	Fuels	Nonfuel
Natural resource–poor countries										
Israel	1962	6.2	110,386	17,709	45,179	46,534	83.1	1.9	0.6	1.3
Turkey	1951	65.3	199,267	3,052	51,148	62,190	56.9	3.9	0.9	3.0
Cyprus	1963	0.8	8,698	11,490	4,151	4,717	101.9	8.9	0.3	8.6
Lebanon*	no	4.3	16,488	3,810	2,141	6,228	50.8	11.3	1.4	9.9
Morocco*	1987	28.7	33,345	1,162	10,453	12,538	68.9	13.2	2.1	11.1
Tunisia*	1990	9.6	19,462	2,035	8,607	9,311	92.1	16.0	15.0	1.0
Intermediate countries										
Jordan*	2000	4.9	8,451	1,729	3,536	5,796	110.4	34.7	0.0	34.7
Egypt*	1970	64.0	98,782	1,544	15,975	22,756	39.2	53.2	48.5	4.7
Bahrain*	1993	0.7	7,971	11,535	6,531	5,056	145.4	67.3	37.1	30.2

Oil-rich countries

Syria*	no	16.2	17,327	1,070	6,846	5,390	70.6	81.7	80.7	1.0
Oman*	no	2.4	14,962	6,247	11,602	6,094	118.3	83.0	82.7	0.3
UAE*	1994	2.9	46,481	16,000	41,270	39,715	174.2	85.1	83.1	2.0
Iraq*	no	23.3	...	...	...	...	...	...	...	...
Iran	no	63.7	101,562	1,595	29,727	17,503	46.5	85.6	85.1	0.5
Yemen*	no	17.5	9,294	531	4,305	3,294	81.8	90.0	89.4	0.6
Saudi Arabia*	no	20.7	173,287	8,362	82,369	53,003	78.1	90.5	90.2	0.3
Qatar*	1994	0.6	14,473	24,744	11,593	3,252	102.6	93.3	93.3	0.0
Algeria*	no	30.4	53,306	1,754	20,813	9,959	57.7	96.3	96.3	0.0
Libya*	no	5.3	27,750	...	6,813	4,914	42.3	96.7	96.6	0.1
Kuwait*	1963	2.0	37,783	19,040	21,203	11,374	86.5	68.3	66.8	1.5
All countries	...	369.3	999,075	2,705	384,359	329,623	71.5	...	...	...
GAFTA	...	233.4	579,162	2,481	254,154	198,680	78.2	...	...	...

Sources: International Monetary Fund, *International Financial Statistics*, 2000; World Bank, *World Development Indicators*, 2001; United Nations Comtrade database.

a. * Denotes GAFTA members.

b. At current exchange rates.

c. For Algeria, Qatar, and UAE, data on services are not available, so numbers reflect goods only.

d. Ratio of the sum of imports and exports to GDP.

Table 6-2. *Product Concentration and Differentiation of Exports*

Country	Percent of SITC items exported[a]		Index of concentration[b]		Intra-industry trade index[b]		Percent of components in total industrial trade, 2000	
	1980	1997	1980	1997	1988	2000	Imports	Exports
Natural resource–poor countries								
Israel	0.84	0.84	0.26	0.28	0.64	0.62	19.5	19.0
Turkey	0.79	0.93	0.23	0.10	0.22	0.31	12.5	3.9
Cyprus	0.50	0.46	0.15	0.15	0.22	0.32	12.8	3.1
Lebanon	0.81	0.67	0.16	0.13	0.26	0.18	11.8	3.5
Morocco	0.42	0.66	0.32	0.18	0.14	0.24	19.2	2.5
Tunisia	0.53	0.75	0.48	0.21	0.23	0.29	14.4	7.4
Intermediate countries								
Jordan	0.45	0.47	0.35	0.27	0.09	0.16	18.4	8.5
Egypt	0.33	0.68	0.57	0.28	0.07	0.18	24.7	3.1
Bahrain	0.24	0.45	0.79	0.63	0.24	0.18	16.5	6.9

Oil-rich countries

Syria	0.44	0.45	0.63	0.56	0.03	0.11	7.6	0.4
Oman	0.42	0.61	0.92	0.72	0.25	0.14	18.8	14.0
UAE	0.82	0.88	0.87	0.62	0.11	0.22	20.8	10.9
Iran	0.37	0.72	0.81	0.80	0.02	0.08	25.6	2.2
Yemen					0.02	0.03	19.6	6.7
Saudi Arabia	0.77	0.73	0.94	0.74	0.13	0.13	19.0	7.1
Qatar	0.01	0.30	0.93	0.73	0.04	0.07	20.4	3.7
Libya	0.18	0.12	0.96	0.77	0.03	0.04	21.3	1.6
Kuwait	0.79	0.65	0.72	0.56	0.06	0.07	17.0	3.9

Memo items

Malaysia	0.85	0.94	0.30	0.19	0.58	0.64	23.1	22.5
Korea	0.85	0.92	0.09	0.14	0.40	0.57	17.6	18.3
Taiwan	0.87	0.93	0.12	0.12	0.43	0.57	17.1	24.3

Sources: United Nations Commission on Trade and Development (UNCTAD), *Handbook of Trade Statistics*, 1997 and 2000; United Nations Comtrade database.

a. Items with "substantial" exports.

b. See text and footnotes for definition of indexes.

(SITC) and the Herfindhal-Hirschmann index (HHI).[16] As expected, oil-rich countries have concentration indices that are much higher than those of natural resource–poor countries—reflecting the concentration in oil (ores) and oil-derived exports permitted by their very strong comparative advantage in fuels. However, this generalization requires some qualification. UAE and Saudi Arabia have relatively diverse exports, reflecting entrepôt activity as well as processing and light manufacturing activities in UAE and the chemical sector in Saudi Arabia. Note also that the number of product categories exported increased substantially for some oil exporters, for example, Qatar. The shares of intermediate or resource-poor Arab countries are below those of their Asian comparators, suggesting a narrower industrial base.

In a number of countries, especially Egypt, Morocco, and Tunisia, there has been a significant diversification of the export base as measured by the SITC indicator. Indeed, on average, the last two decades have seen trade in the region become less concentrated. The HHI suggests that this trend is more general than the SITC measure does—concentration appears to have been falling pretty much across the board. In the case of oil-rich countries this reflects the oil price decline that occurred during this period, which made the production of fuels less profitable compared with the production of oil-derivatives or other goods. But for a number of countries, especially those poor in resources or less endowed with oil, it reflects the pursuit of domestic reforms. Egypt registered a particularly large increase in diversification, rising from 33 to 68 percent on the SITC diversification measure, while the HHI fell from 0.58 to 0.28. Similarly large reductions in the HHI occurred in Morocco and Tunisia.

Table 6-2 also presents data on the magnitude of intra-industry trade.[17] The higher the intra-industry trade (IIT) index, the more the trade of a

16. The SITC is a UN statistical classification for international trade. There are 239 different SITC items at the three-digit level. The SITC measure of concentration is defined as the ratio between the number of three-digit items for which exports exceed US$100,000 and the total number of three-digit items; for small countries an additional criterion of at least a 0.3 percent share in total exports is used. The HHI is defined as the sum of the squares of the market share of each export item in total exports. The lower the HHI is, the less concentrated exports are. The HHI is calculated at the three-digit SITC level.

17. The index is defined as $IIT = 1 - [\Sigma\Sigma\Sigma\, X_{ijk} - M_{ijk} / (X_{ijk} + M_{ijk})]$, where X_{ijk} represents the exports of products from industry i from country j to country k, and M_{ijk} represents the imports of products from industry i by country j from country k. In this study industries are defined at the three-digit level of the SITC.

country involves the exchange of different varieties of a similar type of product. IIT indices of Arab countries are far below those registered by their Asian comparators, which have IIT indices in the 60 percent range. Among Arab countries, Tunisia has the highest intensity of IIT (30 percent), followed by Morocco and UAE. The magnitude of intra-industry trade has been growing rapidly in a number of other countries, however, especially Egypt and Jordan. Oil-rich countries exhibit very low IIT indices, due to their comparative advantage in a limited number of products. UAE is an exception, reflecting its entrepôt trading activity.

Finally, table 6-2 presents data on the share of parts and components in total manufactured exports and imports. This indicator provides information on the relative importance of assembly activity in total trade. A high share of components in imports combined with a low share of components in exports is observed in all Arab countries, except Oman. This compares with much higher ratios and more balanced trade for dynamic exporters in East Asia (table 6-2). For countries with relatively high GDP per capita (interpreted as a proxy for relatively high wages), a combination of a high import share of components and a low export share suggests a high level of assembly activity for domestic or neighboring markets and hence a relatively high degree of effective protection against imports of final (assembled) products. Such activity often is a source of large rents for wholesalers or retailers that are able to import for local assembly. This also may prevail in countries with lower per capita GDP, but a low share of components in exports could also mean that these countries are used as assembly centers for reexport of assembled goods. However, data on outward processing trade collected by the EC suggests that this is not the case.

To summarize: most Arab countries tend to have relatively concentrated exports, although this has been changing rapidly for some nations (Egypt, Morocco, Tunisia); there are low levels of intra-industry trade; and there is a high ratio of imports to exports of components. This suggests important assembly activity directed at domestic markets that are likely to require high protection against imports.

Political Economy Implications of Intra-Arab Trade Patterns

The geographical pattern of exports of Arab countries mirrors what has been said about export structure by product. The share of exports going to other Arab countries ranges from 0.9 (Kuwait) to 13.1 percent (Oman) for oil-rich countries, mirroring the production concentration of these countries (their comparative advantage in the world markets) and the fact that oil is consumed everywhere in the world (table 6-3). For the largest oil producer/exporter, Saudi Arabia, the share is only 7.6 percent. The core set of countries that tend to trade substantially with other Arab countries (around 20 percent or more of total exports) is limited to Jordan, Lebanon, and Syria (some 34, 45 and 18 percent of total exports, respectively). Regional exports account for less than 10 percent of total exports for all other Arab countries, with the exception of Oman.[18]

An important policy question concerning Arab economic integration is whether these levels of intraregional trade are too low because of barriers to trade. An often-used index of the intensity of regional trade is helpful in determining whether the value of trade between two countries is more or less than would be expected on the basis of their importance in world trade. Identification of bilateral combinations in which trade is below expected levels also can help to identify the existence of major barriers to trade. Table 6-4 reports data on the intensity of trade.[19] Values below or above unity indicate that trade between two countries is lower or higher than would be expected. The data suggest that intra-Arab trade flows are not consistently lower than expected—the only countries that trade less with other Arab countries than expected are Algeria and Kuwait. The share of Egypt's exports to the region is about three times larger than expected. Trade intensity indices for Jordan and Lebanon are the highest, followed by the index for Syria. The intensity index for intraregional trade overall is more than double the expected level.

A criticism of intensity indexes is that they do not control for factors such as GDP and trade costs as determinants of trade flows. A commonly used technique to incorporate such factors is the gravity model.[20] Gravity

18. There is some uncertainty on the direction of trade given weak reporting by several countries.

19. The trade intensity index is defined as the share of one country's exports going to a partner divided by the share of world exports going to the partner. That is, $TI_{ij} = [x_{ij} / X_{it}] \div [x_{wj} / X_{wt}]$, where x_{ij} is the value of i's exports to j, and x_{wj} is the value of world exports to j; X_{it} is i's total exports, and X_{wt} is total world exports. An index of more or less than unity indicates a bilateral trade flow that is larger or smaller, respectively, than expected given the partner country's importance in world trade.

20. The gravity model explains bilateral trade between country i and country j. Normally, the amount of trade is directly proportional to size (income, population, land area, and so forth) and inversely proportional to the distance between trading partners i and j. It is

model regressions on *non-oil* trade for the period 1970–98 suggest that in the 1970s, being located in the Middle East and North Africa region had no effect on bilateral trade volumes.[21] In 1980, Arab countries' trade was actually less than predicted by the model. In 1990 and 1998 this pattern reversed, with intra-Arab exports and imports becoming larger than predicted by the model. Research by Al-Atrash and Yousef concludes that while intraregional trade in the Maghreb and among the Gulf Cooperation Council states is less than predicted, that is not true for the Mashreq countries.[22] Therefore the available evidence is somewhat ambiguous on the question of whether intraregional trade flows are lower than would be expected given levels of GDP, population, and geography. Simple shares and trade intensity indexes suggest that intraregional trade is not that low and has been expanding; the gravity regressions suggest that trade is less than expected. However, there has been a noticeable change in the last ten years, with trade now being larger than predicted by the standard gravity model. (See appendix 6A for a brief discussion of trends in bilateral trade over the past thirty years.)

Two questions that are particularly relevant to the prospects of trade-led Arab economic integration deserve attention. First, to what extent do Arab countries that export a lot to the rest of the region (relative to their total exports) also *account for* a major share of intra-Arab exports? Second, how important are exports to other Arab nations in GDP terms for individual Arab countries? The first question captures the balance between each country's incentives to go to a hypothetical regional Arab economic integration conference and its capacity to influence the outcome of such a conference. The second question provides a very rough sense of the importance of intra-Arab trade for the national economy of each prospective member. It can be seen as a crude indicator of the strength of domestic political support for a regional Arab trade option. Despite appearances, trade policy is fundamentally a *domestic* policy—that is, a set of domestic bargains between conflicting domestic interests. This perspective suggests that it is important to ask whether there exists within key Arab countries a sufficiently large

---

expressed by the following equation: $T_{ij} = AY_i^{\beta 1} P_i^{\beta 2} Y_j^{\gamma 1} P_j^{\gamma 2} D_{ij}^{\delta}$, where T is the amount of trade between two trading countries, Y is the GDP of the country, P is the population, and D is the distance between the trading partners. Additional variables, such as existence of a common border or language, are often also included as explanatory variables.

21. Chang (2000).
22. Al-Atrash and Yousef (2000).

Table 6-3. *Geographic Destination of Exports, 2000*

Country	World (US$ millions)	Industrial countries				Percent of total exports — Nonindustrial countries						
		All	Europe	North America	Asia and Pacific	All	Africa	Asia	Europe	Arab nations	Latin America	Not specified
Algeria	20,468	83.4	66.7	16.5	0.2	16.6	1.3	0.8	6.2	1.1	8.2	0.0
Bahrain	5,701	16.8	6.9	5.6	4.4	83.2	3.4	27.4	0.6	9.7	0.2	42.1
Cyprus	953	39.6	36.9	2.4	0.2	60.4	2.5	2.8	15.6	26.1	0.3	11.8
Egypt	5,633	61.1	43.8	14.9	2.4	38.9	2.6	11.2	4.5	9.7	1.0	10.8
Iran	28,345	43.7	25.6	0.9	17.3	56.3	0.0	30.0	3.9	7.5	0.2	14.7
Israel	31,910	69.6	28.6	37.7	3.4	30.4	1.5	15.3	4.3	0.3	2.9	6.1
Jordan	1,897	6.8	2.6	3.4	0.8	93.2	3.3	22.0	1.2	33.8	0.3	33.9
Kuwait	17,752	55.9	14.6	15.2	26.1	44.1	0.1	41.8	0.9	0.9	0.5	0.0
Lebanon	715	36.2	27.0	8.0	1.3	63.8	6.7	4.2	6.9	45.2	0.6	1.4
Libya	12,688	88.2	88.1	0.0	0.1	11.8	2.7	0.5	7.5	3.3	0.2	0.1
Morocco	8,228	73.6	62.7	5.9	3.7	19.0	1.3	8.5	3.3	4.4	2.4	7.4
Oman	10,542	22.5	1.3	2.5	18.8	77.5	0.9	63.4	0.0	13.1	0.0	0.0
Qatar	11,527	51.0	1.1	3.7	46.3	49.0	0.8	31.9	0.1	6.3	0.1	9.8
Saudi Arabia	74,688	54.9	17.9	18.2	18.8	45.1	2.6	32.9	1.2	7.6	1.5	0.0
Syria	4,981	63.5	59.6	3.5	0.3	36.5	1.1	1.5	13.7	18.1	0.2	3.0
Tunisia	5,986	80.2	79.1	0.8	0.3	16.0	3.4	2.5	1.7	8.9	0.9	3.1
Turkey	27,768	66.4	53.4	11.9	1.0	33.6	3.2	2.9	11.2	9.5	1.0	5.6
UAE	41,068	42.0	5.1	2.4	34.5	58.0	1.7	32.6	0.8	9.7	0.2	13.3
Yemen Rep.	4,076	12.3	2.4	6.2	3.8	87.7	1.9	76.2	1.1	4.2	1.6	2.7
Total	314,926	56.3	28.8	12.5	15.0	43.4	1.8	24.4	3.4	6.9	1.5	6.1
All developing countries	2,075,378	53.9	23.7	17.2	13.0	46.1	1.7	28.7	6.3	5.0	4.2	0.1

Source: IMF, *International Financial Statistics*, 2001.

Table 6-4. *Trade Intensity Indexes for Exports from Middle Eastern and North African Countries, 2000*[a]

| Country | All | Industrial countries | | | Developing countries | |
		Europe	North America	Asia and Pacific	Asia	Arab countries
Algeria	1.25	1.77	0.74	0.03	0.04	0.40
Bahrain	0.25	0.18	0.25	0.66	1.56	3.54
Cyprus	0.59	0.98	0.11	0.03	0.16	9.52
Egypt	0.92	1.16	0.67	0.36	0.64	3.52
Iran	0.66	0.68	0.04	2.61	1.71	2.72
Israel	1.04	0.76	1.69	0.51	0.87	0.12
Jordan	0.10	0.07	0.15	0.12	1.26	12.34
Kuwait	0.84	0.39	0.68	3.95	2.38	0.32
Lebanon	0.54	0.71	0.36	0.19	0.24	16.47
Libya	1.32	2.33	0.00	0.01	0.03	1.22
Morocco	1.10	1.66	0.27	0.56	0.48	1.60
Oman	0.34	0.03	0.11	2.84	3.62	4.79
Qatar	0.77	0.03	0.16	7.00	1.82	2.31
Saudi Arabia	0.82	0.47	0.82	2.84	1.88	2.77
Syria	0.95	1.58	0.16	0.05	0.09	6.59
Tunisia	1.20	2.09	0.04	0.04	0.14	3.26
Turkey	1.00	1.42	0.54	0.15	0.16	3.48
UAE	0.63	0.13	0.11	5.21	1.86	3.53
Yemen Rep.	0.18	0.06	0.28	0.57	4.34	1.54
Average of all listed	0.85	0.76	0.56	2.27	1.39	2.52

Source: Authors' calculations based on IMF, *International Financial Statistics,* 2001.
a. See text and footnotes for definition of index.

domestic coalition in favor of regional trade, and the importance of the question is amplified when it is recognized that a country has alternatives to regional trade. Many Arab countries already are pursuing discriminatory agreements with one large industrial country or more. A significant number of countries have signed Euro-Mediterranean partnership agreements with the EC. And, of course, many are members of the WTO and have the option of pursuing multilateral liberalization.

All of the Arab countries that have substantial exports to other Arab nations (more than $1 billion)—Oman, Saudi Arabia, and the UAE—are oil exporters. These three countries account for almost 60 percent of total intra-Arab trade. As already mentioned, with the exception of Oman, in

Table 6-5. *Intra-Arab Export Shares and Weight in GDP, 2000*

Country	Value of exports to Arab countries (US$ millions)	Percent of total Arab trade	Exports to Arab countries as percent of total exports	Exports to Arab countries as a percent of GDP
Algeria	224	1.2	1.1	0.4
Bahrain	554	3.0	9.7	7.0
Egypt	544	2.9	9.7	0.6
Iran	2,117	11.3	7.5	2.0
Jordan	642	3.4	33.8	7.7
Kuwait	154	0.8	0.9	0.4
Lebanon	323	1.7	45.2	2.0
Libya	425	2.3	3.3	1.4
Morocco	360	1.9	4.4	1.1
Oman	1,386	7.4	13.1	7.0
Qatar	731	3.9	6.3	5.1
Saudi Arabia	5,680	30.3	7.6	3.3
Syria	900	4.8	18.1	5.3
Tunisia	535	2.9	8.9	2.7
UAE	3,981	21.3	9.7	8.3
Yemen Rep.	172	0.9	4.2	2.0
Total	18,728	100.0	7.4	2.7

Source: IMF, *International Financial Statistics*, 2001; World Bank, *World Development Indicators*, 2001.

none of them do intraregional exports account for more than 10 percent of the country's total exports (table 6-5). In the case of Oman and UAE, those exports are equivalent to 7 to 8 percent of GDP and include more than oil and oil derivatives, suggesting that there may be significant political support for Arab economic integration in these countries. However, it should be recognized that they are not large countries in the regional context and therefore have only limited capacity to push such an initiative forward. Countries with a high share of their total exports going to the Arab region—such as Jordan, Lebanon, and Syria—represent only a small share of total intra-Arab trade (3, 2, and 5 percent, respectively), implying that their potential influence in a regional trade process also is likely to be small.

In addition to Oman and the UAE, there are three other countries whose exports to Arab countries constitute more than 5 percent of their GDP:

Bahrain, Jordan, and Syria. This is not insignificant and suggests that those countries may have an interest in pursuing Arab economic integration. The figure for Saudi Arabia is 3.3 percent; for Tunisia, 2.7 percent; and for the other countries, less than 2 percent of GDP.

These numbers suggest that the situation is significantly different from that prevailing at the creation of the EC. In the mid-1950s, all prospective EC member states exported more than 25 percent of their total exports to the rest of the community. Intra-Arab trade shares are much lower for almost all Arab countries. Moreover, EC trade amounted to more than 3 percent of domestic GDP for future EC member states (5 percent for Germany), with Italy, at 2.8 percent, being the only exception. While the Arab trade/GDP ratios for many countries are similar, an important difference is that the variance is much higher for a number of countries, including Egypt. For Egypt, which would have to be an important member of any integration initiative, the ratio is quite low. Of possible trade agreements, Arab integration is therefore less attractive.

To summarize: the available data suggest that intra-Arab trade is not less than would be expected given fundamentals, especially for non-Maghreb countries; economies that sell a large share of their exports to the region (the potential core supporters of Arab economic integration) account for small shares of total intra-Arab trade; conversely, such trade accounts for only a small share of total exports of countries that account for a large share of total intra-Arab trade; and there is a large variance in the magnitude of intra-Arab trade as a share of domestic GDP in Arab countries. All of this suggests that the political economy of Arab integration based on preferential merchandise trade liberalization is not propitious.

Toward a Services-Based Integration Strategy?

What are possible alternatives? An obvious option is to focus on other markets, including factor markets—labor, investment—and services. Reforms in service sector policies to reduce domestic production and trade costs are needed in their own right. They also may have a high payoff in facilitating further liberalization of trade in goods by enhancing the ability of firms to compete on world markets.

Services-related costs are high in many Arab countries. As far as trade is concerned, logistics-related costs often are high due to government policies and regulations that result in limited competition. Public monopolies in ports and port services combined with poor infrastructure for loading and storing goods make the costs for discharging a container two to three times higher in Alexandria than in other Mediterranean ports. Port service charges in Arab countries can reach up to 10 percent of the value of imported intermediate components.[23] Monopoly shipping and domestic policies favoring national carriers result in low-quality, low-frequency, and high-cost services. Similar observations can be made for air transportation, telecommunications, and utilities. Policies restricting trade in land transport services—such as prohibitions on drivers originating in certain countries, arbitrary changes in documentary requirements, surcharges and discriminatory taxes, and prohibitions on obtaining return cargo in the country of destination to take back to the country of origin—impose severe costs on intra-Arab trade.[24]

More generally, inefficient services place a substantial burden on the manufacturing and agricultural sectors. Services—ranging from financial intermediation and insurance to the design and marketing of products and access to high-quality, low-cost telecommunications—are a major determinant of the competitiveness of firms. Because services often are not tradable, service sector liberalization involves a mix of deregulation—dismantling barriers to entry (investment) and promoting competition—and re-regulation—establishing an improved legal environment and strengthening specialized and independent regulatory agencies. The limited tradability of services implies that FDI is an important avenue for acquiring access to best practices and new services. Given that many service activities are subject to investment restrictions (for example, nationality requirements, restrictions on movement of personnel, limits on foreign equity shareholding), service sector reform is closely tied to privatization and the removal of licensing and related entry and operating restrictions.

Arab countries have tended to approach service sector reform in a piecemeal fashion. Privatization has been slower than in other parts of the world; barriers to entry often remain forbidding, both for domestic and foreign investors; and there are few independent regulatory agencies to ensure that markets are contestable. Privatization proceeds generated in the Arab region

23. Cassing and others (2000).
24. Zarrouk (2000).

constituted only 3 percent of the worldwide total in the 1990s. While the trend is increasing—rising from some $22 million in the early 1990s to $2 billion in 1995 to more than $6 billion in the second half of the 1990s—the role of the state remains much higher than in other regions.[25] Private sector participation in infrastructure is very limited. Between 1984 and 1997, projects in the region added up to only $9 billion, compared with a worldwide total of $650 billion, for a share of just 1.4 percent.[26] Given the inefficient operation and management of state-owned and -controlled utilities, there is an urgent need to move to a sector-wide approach that includes a combination of competition, incentive-based regulation, and private ownership.[27]

Because services often cannot be traded, increasing access to domestic service markets is likely to require the entry of foreign competitors through FDI. This will have two effects: a reduction in what Konan and Maskus call the cartel effect—the markup of price over marginal cost that incumbents are able to charge due to restricted entry—and an attenuation of what they call the cost inefficiency effect—the fact that in an environment with limited competition incumbents' marginal costs are likely to be higher than if entry were allowed.[28] Procompetitive reforms can then have a major impact on economic performance as many services are critical inputs into production. Moreover, in sharp contrast to what happens with merchandise liberalization, liberalization of services (FDI or domestic) generates demand for *domestic* labor. Foreign banks, retailers, or telecommunications operators all need local labor. Thus, while the deregulation of entry inevitably will result in the restructuring of domestic industry, service sector reform has fewer far-reaching implications for sectoral turnover and aggregate sectoral employment than the abolition of trade barriers for merchandise. The simulation analysis undertaken by Konan suggests that reforms in services are less demanding in terms of labor adjustment than liberalization of trade in merchandise.[29]

25. Economic Research Forum (2001).

26. Examples of recent initiatives include water supply and wastewater treatment (Oman), power (Egypt, Morocco, Tunisia, and several GCC countries), transport (a port terminal in Yemen and a container terminal in Oman; toll roads in Jordan, Lebanon, Morocco, and Tunisia; and port services in Morocco and Tunisia), and telecommunications (the GCC countries, Jordan, Lebanon, and Morocco). See Economic Research Forum (2001).

27. Economic Research Forum (2001).

28. Konan and Maskus (2002).

29. Konan, chapter 5 of this volume.

Service sector reform also can have a large indirect payoff by generating political support for and thus facilitating merchandise trade liberalization. Trade barriers are still high in the region, not only because of tariffs but also a variety of nontariff measures that raise trade costs.[30] As a result there remains substantial anti-export bias in many Arab countries.[31] Traditional (nondiscriminatory) trade liberalization therefore remains a priority. One reason progress in this area has been slow is that liberalization will invariably result in contraction or adjustment of domestic industries that benefit from protection, while industries in which the country has a comparative advantage will expand. Many of the latter initially are likely to be small and dispersed, whereas the former are likely to be concentrated. Thus the well-known political problem of building support for trade liberalization—those that stand to lose often have a substantially stronger political voice as they have more information and more incentive to organize. Frequently it will not be known beforehand which sectors and activities will become growth areas—hence an additional lag between those who will lose and those who will gain from liberalization. This makes the early transition process politically difficult, and it can impede liberalization.

Political constraints to trade liberalization may be overcome if reforms target the service sector. Such reforms can lower trade-related transport, logistics, and transaction costs and reduce the cost and increase the variety of key inputs such as finance, telecommunications, marketing, distribution, and similar services. Procompetitive reforms that facilitate entry by new firms also will generate employment opportunities for skilled and unskilled workers who currently are employed by government or import-competing private manufacturers or who are unemployed. Indeed, a political precondition for public sector downsizing is that such alternative employment opportunities emerge. Fears of employment loss need to be addressed beforehand through the establishment of safety nets and transitional adjustment assistance, but what matters most is that employment opportunities are created elsewhere in the regional economy following reform. A major benefit of a concerted strategy toward service sector reform is that it will in

---

30. Zarrouk, chapter 4 of this volume.
31. Galal and Fawzy, chapter 3 of this volume.

itself generate greater demand for labor by the private sector—whether in services or goods-producing industries.[32]

A central issue is the rationale for pursuing services, trade, and investment liberalization in the regional context. Much of what is needed could be pursued through unilateral action. Indeed, in other work we have argued that in general the need for reciprocal exchange of policy commitments should be much less necessary in the area of services than in merchandise trade liberalization.[33] This is supported by recent experience in many parts of the world, especially Latin America and eastern Europe, where great progress has been made since the late 1980s to privatize and increase competition in the service sector. A feature of many of these efforts has been that reforms were pursued as part of programs to address major macroeconomic crises—situations that have not arisen in the Arab context. The limited progress in addressing services-related trade costs and expanding competition and private participation in backbone infrastructure services in Arab countries suggests that there are political economy factors that impede pro-competitive, unilateral reforms.[34] A key question is whether and how an Arab integration-based effort to liberalize services can help overcome national political constraints to reform.

A possible rationale for regional cooperation in the service sector could revolve around regulatory economies of scale or scope. Another is that it could be a mechanism for governments to make credible commitments to reform. Only if there is a credible commitment will manufacturing and other interest groups have the incentive to invest resources and political capital in supporting the implementation of service sector reform and to resist backsliding. Concerted action in the context of an Arab economic integration initiative could facilitate the credibility of reform by creating focal points (benchmarks or targets); mobilizing the needed high-level attention and engagement by senior decisionmakers, political leaders, and civil society; and providing a mechanism to lock in a reform path through a commitment to specific targets or outcomes.

---

32. Markusen, Rutherford, and Tarr (2002).

33. Hoekman and Messerlin (2000).

34. It is also illustrative that only Algeria, Kuwait, Tunisia, and Turkey currently have (weak) competition laws and that efforts to adopt such legislation in Egypt, Jordan, and Morocco have proved contentious.

A necessary condition for credibility is that the Arab cooperation strategy must help to address major political constraints that impede unilateral reform. One of these relates to the large role of the state in many Arab economies. Greater participation by the private sector will require privatization and the abolition of entry restrictions for new firms. Government policies and procedures (red tape) also cause high transaction costs at the border. Therefore a major factor in the relevance of any integration strategy will be the extent to which governments use it to pre-commit themselves to actions to reduce the role of the state. This implies that the focus must be on *government services* as well as backbone infrastructure, both hard and soft. Two interest groups play a major role in this regard—government employees in general and, more specifically, those responsible for enforcement of regulatory policies and procedures at the border (customs) and in specific service industries (sectoral regulators).

Cross-country experience suggests that the latter group can be a serious constraint on the adoption of more procompetitive policies. Sectoral ministries or regulators that oversee service industries often will be more concerned with supporting domestic incumbents and maintaining the status quo, having little incentive to actively encourage new entry and greater competition, whether from domestic or foreign suppliers. The bureaucratic incentives confronting sectoral regulators generally imply that little weight is put on the economywide dimensions of policies.

The resulting entry barriers often create significant rents for incumbents, who have a strong interest in blocking attempts to increase the contestability of "their" markets. It is important to ensure that potential entrants are free to enter service markets and that policies do not discriminate against foreign in favor of domestic entrants. Entry barriers in many service activities tend to be justified by invoking market-failure rationales that revolve around information asymmetries, fears of excessive entry, the need for universal service, and so forth. While often there is a valid rationale for regulation, it generally does not require the creation of legal barriers to entry.

Regional cooperation can assist in the removal of national entry barriers by providing a focal point for reform and mechanisms to monitor progress. In addition, there also are potential regulatory economies that can arise. One element of cooperation could be the establishment of regional regulatory agencies to oversee network services (telecommunications, electricity, railways, and other critical backbone activities) and to "de-balkanize" Arab markets for such services. Regional regulatory agencies could facilitate cooperation between Arab countries that are investing in and managing the physical networks by issuing regionwide licenses for a market large enough to attract global players. A regional effort to create a common competition authority may help to identify private collusive arrangements and public policies that restrict competition in regional markets.

The sequencing of reforms will be important to making and sustaining progress. One possibility is to start with a regional effort on trade facilitation (broadly defined to include key government services that influence trade transactions costs), followed by initiatives to promote more effective competition on the regional market for network-type service industries and to liberalize entry into markets through investment (establishment). Starting with trade facilitation puts pressure on only a small subset of the civil service and benefits foreign and domestic producers equally. Red tape costs represent social waste—they do not generate revenue or rents. Consequently, reducing those costs can benefit the economy substantially.

As documented by Zarrouk in chapter 4, trade costs in the region are high, in part because of government restrictions and controls at the border and in part because of a lack of competition in port, transport, and related services. High trade costs are generally recognized as a priority by the private sector. Regional cooperation could help governments move forward by setting quantitative benchmarks for improvement, establishing mileposts, and creating transparency and oversight mechanisms to monitor the progress achieved. Cross-country experience suggests that moving forward to facilitate trade by addressing regulatory and logistics restraints requires the engagement of high-level political authorities, something that is difficult to sustain. A regional initiative could help ensure that the necessary attention and support is provided over time, as the reforms needed generally take a substantial amount of time as well as resources for training, upgrading of hardware and infrastructure, and so forth.

To the greatest extent technically possible, regional initiatives should aim to reduce costs for all trade and all traders, irrespective of origin. The primary rationale for undertaking this effort in a concerted fashion is to create clear focal points and objectives and to mobilize the high-level support needed to make progress. There is no rationale for differentiating between goods of Arab and other origin; trade facilitation should apply on a most-favored-nation basis. The same applies to service sector reforms more generally; they should be applied on a nondiscriminatory basis.

A second potential area for regional cooperation is to develop mechanisms to increase the contestability of markets, especially for backbone infrastructure services. Examples of cooperation could involve the establishment of regional regulatory agencies to oversee network services (telecommunications, electricity, railways, and other critical backbone activities). These agencies could facilitate cooperation between Arab countries that are investing in and managing the physical networks by issuing region-wide licenses for a market that would be large enough to attract global players. Arab economic integration could also be a vehicle through which regional competition disciplines are agreed on and enforced to prevent private collusive arrangements and public policies that impede entry or restrict competition in regional markets.

A regional effort to liberalize backbone services could start with defining the "relevant market" in a more appropriate way. For instance, liberalizing air transport without liberalizing airport slots does not lead very far: the price of air travel will mirror both competitive pressures in terms of routes (if there are several airlines, which is not necessarily the case) and monopoly rents related to airport slot monopolies. The same is true for maritime transport: Francois and Wooton estimate that the welfare gains from trade liberalization—better access to markets—may be doubled if complementary actions are taken to increase competition in the shipping sector.[35] These are all examples of the types of interactions that tend to be ignored by national sectoral regulators and could be addressed more efficiently in a regionwide approach.

Lessons from the EC Experience

The EC experience suggests that careful consideration needs to be given to the design and sequencing of regional cooperation on service sector policy. Although a central pillar of the EC integration strategy was preferential merchandise trade liberalization, a common external trade policy, and com-

35. Francois and Wooton (2000).

mon management of agriculture, the EC also covers services and factor flows (investment and movement of workers).[36] A number of lessons can be drawn from the EC experience.

First, there must be an overarching vision of the ultimate objective of the exercise. Second, a clear path or strategy to achieve the objectives must be developed. Third, the implementation of the strategy must result in an overall balance of gains for members at any point in time. This will require flexibility and may imply a need to carve out some sectors from the liberalization objective, as agriculture was by the EC. Rather than simply exempting "difficult" sectors from the ambit of the customs union, the EC brought them under the umbrella of the integration goal through a common policy that was administered by EC institutions. To a significant extent, the joint management of these common policies became the focus of day-to-day interaction at the community level and helped make the EC a reality for national bureaucracies and stakeholders. In addition, the EC developed transfer mechanisms to redistribute income to disadvantaged groups and regions. Finally, the supranational nature of the EC was important in maintaining the venture over time—a self-interested bureaucracy that was given a mandate to pursue integration proved very effective at mobilizing support for new initiatives, while enforcement of the rules of the game was pursued through the independent European Court of Justice.

The EC experience illustrates that engaging in regional cooperation to liberalize trade and investment in services is hard. The Common Market was limited to goods—although the manufacturing sector accounted for less than one-third of EC GDP. Most services, which represented the lion's share of GDP, were left untouched by intra-EC liberalization until the 1990s. In part, this reflected the fact that many service providers in the EC were public monopolies or firms to which member states granted special or exclusive rights. While these were subject to specific treaty provisions regarding state-owned enterprises and state aids, only in the late 1980s did

---

36. Another option is to focus on liberalization of trade in factors of production, something that is not discussed in this paper. Trade in labor services has traditionally been relatively important among Arab countries, albeit hampered by significant barriers and high transactions costs (Schiff 1996). There are close links between temporary movement of people and liberalization of trade in services. What is required in the case of labor services is primarily a relaxation of quantitative restrictions—imposed through visas and economic needs tests and investment controls.

EC member states begin to embark on a major effort to privatize and introduce regulatory reform of trade in services. Following Article 52 (formerly 63), the EC focused primarily on only a limited number of services— those perceived as constituting the infrastructure backbone of the economy: financial services, telecommunications, and transport by land, air, and sea.[37] The late 1990s witnessed painful and not always successful efforts to extend the list to electronic commerce, electricity and natural gas services, railways, and postal services.

In the Arab context, it is very difficult to assess beforehand which sectors will be sensitive, where there are common interests, and what the balance is of national gains and potential losses (adjustment costs). This will require detailed analysis and extensive political debate and discussion. However, a case can be made that national interests regarding service sector reforms should be relatively balanced. In all countries, many industries stand to benefit significantly from service sector liberalization and policy reform. Manufacturers and agricultural producers should have a strong interest in seeing their input costs decline and the variety and quality of available services increase. They can therefore be expected to be a powerful force supporting regulatory reform in services *if* a credible case can be made that the integration effort will result in such an outcome.

That will require eliminating entry barriers created by explicit discrimination (for example, no right of establishment and FDI) and regulatory differences that result in market segmentation. Doing so in a cooperative manner is difficult. Perhaps the most powerful force that can be unleashed through integration is to increase competition by relaxing entry constraints—explicit barriers rather than the implicit ones created by regulatory differences—and adopting mechanisms to discipline state aids and anticompetitive business practices. That would require institutions of the type created by the EC to monitor and challenge the behavior of governments and to address anticompetitive practices of incumbent firms. State aids and intervention, as well as the absence of effective competition legislation, are two important factors in many Arab economies, suggesting that,

---

37. Article 52 reads: "Priority for liberalization shall as a general rule be given to those services which directly affect production costs or the liberalization of which helps to promote trade in goods." It again illustrates the predominance of trade in goods as the focus of the EC process.

in regard to common institutions and disciplines, attention should focus on those areas. Another high-priority area for institutional cooperation and development relates to dispute settlement. As mentioned, the ECJ played a major role in advancing the integration effort in the EC. Without a mechanism to enforce commitments on FDI and entry into services, the effort will inherently be much less credible to the private sector, both inside and outside the region.

The feasibility of moving rapidly to emulate the institutional complexity that prevails in the EC is of course limited. The institutional framework of the EC has grown incrementally, and the same would be true in the Arab context. Cooperation in regulatory areas and common competition policies will undoubtedly emerge only gradually. What matters most in this regard is for all parties to agree on a vision and launch the implementation process. This could encompass possible "half-way houses" that could be used to build support for procompetitive reforms. One option could be a regional mechanism to increase the transparency of government policies, including assessments of the economic effect of regulations and other policies that limit competition. Mechanisms to generate such information, which is necessary to mobilize national constituencies that would be negatively affected by reforms, are discussed in Hoekman and Mavroidis.[38]

Whatever the specific features and modalities of cooperation, the economywide benefits of services reform will be greatest if regional reforms and disciplines are applied on a nondiscriminatory basis. Compared with preferential liberalization of trade in goods, concerted service sector reform is less likely to give rise to serious trade and investment diversion, in that policies often will be applied equally to both foreign (nonregional) and regional suppliers. A reason for that is that regulation should aim to address market failures and thus apply on a nondiscriminatory basis. The same often will be true in practice for policies affecting FDI—the major mode of contesting service markets—which generally do not distinguish between foreign investors on the basis of nationality. However, in principle that certainly can be done, and on the investment front such discrimination is pursued (on paper) in the Arab League through an Arab rule of origin requiring a minimum Arab equity ownership share. It is important that such discrimination be minimized if Arab economic integration is to be beneficial.

38. Hoekman and Mavroidis (2000).

Concluding Remarks

Arab economic integration efforts that revolve around merchandise trade liberalization face substantial impediments: markets are generally small; strong comparative advantages in natural resources generate export concentration and require geographical diversification of exports beyond the region to reduce risk; and major Arab countries do not appear to have strong incentives to take the lead in pursuing merchandise trade–based economic integration, while smaller countries that do have the incentive do not have the influence to ensure implementation. Arab countries confront an incentive structure that is quite different from that prevailing at the creation of the EC in the 1950s, suggesting that emulating the EC approach—which is based on preferential merchandise trade liberalization and creation of a common external merchandise trade policy, leaving service sector reform for later—is unlikely to be a fruitful strategy for Arab countries.

For Arab economic integration efforts to be successful there must be a sufficiently large domestic coalition that favors it over all alternatives.[39] Given the limited magnitude and potential for intra-Arab trade—and thus political support for efforts to expand trade—complementary instruments and approaches are needed. One option discussed is to focus on the service sector—defined to include both government and major backbone infrastructure-type services. Integration efforts that focus on services have the potential to generate gains that would be a multiple of those that could be obtained from preferential merchandise trade liberalization.[40] Indeed, preferential trade liberalization is unlikely to generate significant benefits—the best trade policy strategy for the region is to pursue nondiscriminatory liberalization. The latter is critical for many countries in the region—trade barriers are among the highest in the world outside of South Asia and consequently anti-export bias is strong.

A key question concerns the need for a regional or concerted approach to service sector reform. The incentives to pursue such reforms are large, and other parts of the world have implemented them on a unilateral basis. However, progress in this area has been slower in Arab countries, suggesting

39. Galal (2000).
40. Konan, chapter 5 of this volume.

that there are political economy constraints that are more binding. To become an engine for Arab integration, the joint pursuit of reform will have to be an effective vehicle in helping to overcome political economy resistance to unilateral reforms.

The European experience illustrates that for integration strategies to be successful and to be sustained, powerful constituencies must see them as contributing to the realization of desired objectives. While political objectives were paramount in the EC, their realization involved the identification of economic measures that benefited all citizens, on average, while ensuring that concerns and interests of key blocking coalitions and groups were satisfied. The challenge for supporters of Arab economic integration initiatives will be to identify objectives that are supported by citizens and mechanisms of regional cooperation that can help attain those objectives. Decisionmakers must be able to make a compelling case that "going regional" will generate significant benefits that cannot be realized through unilateral action.

While there certainly is potential for a services-based approach to generating those benefits, it must be recognized that the design and implementation of concerted action will be complex. A major lesson of the EC is that the pursuit of political objectives may come at a high economic cost—the common agricultural policy is an example. A path to integration that focuses on service markets therefore should be designed to minimize the scope for capture by—and creation of—vested interests. In this regard there is less potential for trade diversion under a services-related strategy as regulatory reforms often will be applied on a nondiscriminatory basis. Nondiscriminatory regulation is important, because discriminatory regional regulation may result in economies becoming locked in by less efficient regional suppliers and standards that would impede the ability of more efficient foreign firms to contest the market at a later date even if the discriminatory policy was removed.[41]

41. Mattoo and Fink (2002) discuss a number of issues that affect the sequencing of preferential and multilateral liberalization of services. They point to the potential problem of negative path dependence if preferential liberalization in services occurs for network industries with sunk costs—the end result may be durable entry restrictions against more efficient nonregional suppliers.

Any regional approach to service sector reform must recognize the fact that many Arab countries have signed agreements with the EC and that many also are engaged in negotiations on goods and services trade in the WTO. The Euro-Med agreements all include provisions calling for the development of disciplines for investment (establishment) and trade in services. They also embody numerous provisions calling for the EC to cooperate in providing technical and financial assistance in trade-related regulatory areas. These agreements can and should be taken into account in the design of any Arab integration strategy. Indeed, while the focus here has been on Arab cooperation options, a similar strategy can be pursued in the context of agreements with major high-income economies such as the EC and the United States. Deep integration agreements with such partners may well give rise to greater benefits through enhanced credibility effects and the financial and technical assistance transfers that are likely to be associated with them.[42]

More generally, an Arab services integration and cooperation strategy can and should be anchored in the WTO to ensure that policies are applied on a nondiscriminatory basis wherever possible. Of course, making commitments in the WTO allows concessions to be obtained from trading partners, expanding the potential gains from committing to reform. Given that the focus of negotiations at the WTO is on the depth of policy "bindings," the fruits of regional reforms can be used as negotiating coin. Anchoring domestic liberalization in the WTO also can help Arab countries make reform less prone to backsliding as negatively affected foreign suppliers will oppose domestic efforts to reimpose trade barriers. That said, it must be recognized that WTO negotiations on services have not progressed very far to date, general disciplines on investment and competition policies do not exist, and many of the regulatory service reform priorities remain outside the ambit of the WTO.

Appendix 6A. Trends in Bilateral Trade, 1960–2000

The body of this chapter describes the *current* pattern of trade among countries in the Middle East. It is interesting to complete the picture by examining what has been happening over time to see whether this pattern has always

---

42. World Bank (2000).

existed. A comparison of intraregional bilateral trade flows over the 1964–97 period suggests that there has been a significant decline in the relative importance of intraregional trade since the early 1960s but that it picked up in the 1990s. A matrix of bilateral imports is reported in table 6A-1, with data aggregated according to the natural resource–intensity of trading partners. Table 6A-2 does the same for exports. The region here is defined to include all countries, not just Arab nations.

The data reveal two different types of evolution in imports from Arab economies. On one hand, countries that are not oil-rich witnessed decline or stability in their share of regional trade until 1985, followed by a reversal that generally was not large enough to counterbalance the previous decline. On the other hand, oil-rich countries tended to increase trade with other Arab countries—an evolution that may reveal an income effect: oil-rich countries may have been induced to diversify their purchases because of lower oil prices and to turn toward less expensive local sellers.

In the early 1960s, Lebanon and Jordan imported about 60 percent of all non-oil imports from the region. By 1997, that had dropped to the 10 to 15 percent range. Note that many countries register an increase in the intraregional share of total imports after 1985. Increases are substantial for Syria, Iraq, Oman, Saudi Arabia, Libya, and Kuwait. The regional breakdown of exports also suggests that the long-term trend is down—in 1997 most countries exported less to the region in relative terms than in the early 1960s (table 6A-2). The exceptions with respect to non-oil trade that show a recovery in the last ten to fifteen years include Egypt, Syria, Saudi Arabia, Algeria, Libya, and Kuwait. In the case of Syria, Egypt, and Lebanon, the increase involves non-oil economies, while for Saudi Arabia the increase is in oil-rich countries (suggesting again growth of intra-industry trade in oil-related products).

Table 6A-1. *Intraregional Import Pattern, Selected Years, 1964–97*

Percent of total trade

Country	Natural resource–poor countries 1964	1978	1985	1997	Intermediate countries 1964	1978	1985	1997	Oil-rich countries 1964	1978	1985	1997	Total regional trade 1964	1978	1985	1997
Including oil																
Israel	0.9	0.1	0.2	1.3	0.9	0.0	0.0	0.1	0.1	0.1	0.0	0.0	1.9	0.3	0.2	1.4
Turkey	1.3	2.2	1.0	0.8	1.2	0.9	0.2	0.9	9.3	23.5	31.1	7.6	11.8	26.6	32.4	9.3
Lebanon	3.9	1.4	5.5	3.6	2.6	1.6	1.0	1.1	18.2	12.7	0.8	7.7	24.7	15.6	7.3	12.4
Morocco	0.0	1.1	0.4	1.3	0.4	0.7	0.0	0.3	2.3	8.0	21.5	10.8	2.8	9.8	21.9	12.3
Tunisia	0.2	1.9	1.2	1.8	0.5	0.1	0.4	0.6	5.6	5.3	7.4	5.0	6.3	7.3	9.0	7.4
Jordan	7.5	6.7	4.2	4.6	2.3	1.9	0.5	1.3	12.9	15.4	25.8	21.2	22.6	24.0	30.5	27.1
Egypt	0.5	2.0	1.1	2.0	0.0	0.2	0.2	0.2	5.2	1.9	2.0	4.6	5.7	4.2	3.2	6.8
Bahrain	0.0	0.3	0.6	1.1	0.0	0.0	0.1	0.8	85.7	45.8	48.1	11.7	85.7	46.1	48.8	13.6
Syria	6.6	4.1	2.5	6.8	2.6	3.0	0.6	2.2	8.8	9.6	27.2	5.6	17.9	16.7	30.2	14.6
Oman	0.0	0.5	0.1	0.5	0.0	2.9	0.5	1.0	98.1	16.5	22.4	26.7	98.1	19.9	23.0	28.1
UAE	0.0	1.0	1.7	1.1	0.0	1.4	4.1	0.4	93.3	2.8	4.4	6.3	93.3	5.2	10.1	7.8
Iraq	2.8	1.8	11.7	5.6	1.4	0.9	2.2	15.3	1.8	0.7	0.1	3.1	5.9	3.4	14.0	24.0
Iran	1.1	1.5	11.6	3.1	0.0	0.7	0.0	0.1	3.5	1.0	0.8	2.0	4.6	3.2	12.4	5.2
Yemen	0.0	0.8	0.3	4.2	2.8	0.7	0.4	2.3	76.0	23.4	0.6	7.5	78.9	24.9	1.3	14.0
Saudi Arabia	6.2	1.8	1.8	10.6	5.7	0.8	1.2	0.1	8.0	1.4	1.9	23.3	19.9	4.1	5.0	34.0
Qatar	1.3	1.0	1.5	0.4	0.0	0.7	1.1	0.9	4.6	4.3	5.6	6.4	5.9	6.0	8.2	7.7
Algeria	2.6	0.3	2.3	3.9	0.2	0.1	0.1	0.5	0.2	0.2	0.4	3.4	3.0	0.7	2.8	7.8
Libya	1.4	3.1	4.5	9.5	0.7	0.1	0.0	2.7	0.9	0.2	0.1	1.0	3.0	3.4	4.6	13.3
Kuwait	2.8	2.0	2.2	2.5	1.3	1.0	0.6	1.9	5.4	1.6	0.1	11.4	9.6	4.6	3.0	15.8
Yemen, DR	0.3	0.0	0.0	—	1.0	4.1	0.5	—	40.8	15.0	2.8	—	42.1	19.1	3.3	—

Excluding oil

Israel	0.1	0.1	0.2	1.4	1.7	0.0	0.0	0.1	0.1	0.2	0.0	0.0	1.9	0.3	0.2	1.5
Turkey	1.8	1.2	1.5	0.8	0.3	0.4	0.3	0.3	0.4	0.3	1.0	1.9	2.4	1.9	2.8	3.0
Lebanon	11.4	1.6	5.3	3.9	7.4	1.9	0.5	1.2	41.3	2.1	0.3	4.2	60.2	5.6	6.1	9.3
Morocco	0.0	1.2	0.5	1.5	0.4	0.8	0.1	0.3	0.5	0.1	0.4	3.0	1.0	2.2	0.9	4.8
Tunisia	0.4	2.0	1.1	1.5	0.7	0.1	0.4	0.6	2.5	0.2	1.9	1.9	3.6	2.3	3.4	4.0
Jordan	24.8	7.5	5.4	5.4	8.9	2.1	0.7	1.5	33.4	6.5	5.8	8.7	67.1	16.1	11.9	15.6
Egypt	0.6	2.1	1.0	1.8	0.0	0.2	0.2	0.2	4.4	1.8	1.0	4.1	4.9	4.1	2.1	6.1
Bahrain	0.0	0.5	1.2	1.1	0.1	0.1	0.3	0.8	31.3	5.8	3.9	11.8	31.4	6.3	5.3	13.8
Syria	8.1	4.7	3.5	7.1	3.2	3.5	0.8	2.3	10.0	0.6	0.7	5.2	21.3	8.7	5.0	14.6
Oman	0.0	0.6	0.1	0.5	0.0	0.6	0.1	0.5	96.4	12.9	22.0	25.9	0.0	14.1	22.3	26.9
UAE	0.0	1.1	1.8	1.1	0.0	0.5	0.7	0.4	1.2	0.7	2.8	6.2	1.2	2.2	5.2	7.7
Iraq	1.3	1.8	11.8	5.6	0.7	0.9	2.2	15.3	0.8	0.7	0.1	3.1	2.8	3.4	14.1	24.0
Iran	0.6	1.5	12.3	3.2	0.5	0.5	0.0	0.1	1.2	0.8	0.4	2.0	1.9	2.8	12.7	5.3
Yemen	0.0	0.8	0.3	4.2	15.5	0.6	0.4	1.6	77.0	22.1	0.6	7.5	92.5	23.5	1.4	13.4
Saudi Arabia	1.6	1.8	1.9	10.9	1.5	0.8	1.2	0.1	2.1	1.4	1.9	23.8	5.2	4.1	4.9	34.7
Qatar	0.3	1.0	1.5	0.4	0.0	0.7	1.1	0.9	0.7	4.3	5.5	6.4	1.0	6.0	8.1	7.7
Algeria	2.5	0.3	2.3	4.0	0.2	0.1	0.1	0.5	0.2	0.1	0.4	2.6	2.9	0.5	2.8	7.1
Libya	0.7	3.1	4.6	9.5	0.3	0.1	0.0	2.7	0.3	0.2	0.1	1.0	1.2	3.4	4.7	13.3
Kuwait	1.0	2.0	2.2	2.5	0.5	1.0	0.6	1.9	1.9	1.6	0.1	11.1	3.4	4.6	3.0	15.5
Yemen, DR	0.2	0.1	0.0	—	0.6	0.1	0.6	—	10.8	1.7	0.0	—	11.6	1.9	0.7	—

Source: Authors' calculations based on the UN Comtrade database.

Table 6A-2. *Intraregional Export Pattern, Selected Years, 1964–97*
Percent of total trade

Country	Natural resource-poor countries				Intermediate countries				Oil-rich countries				Total regional trade			
	1964	1978	1985	1997	1964	1978	1985	1997	1964	1978	1985	1997	1964	1978	1985	1997
Including oil																
Israel	1.9	1.8	0.6	1.1	0.0	0.0	0.2	0.4	1.5	2.8	0.0	1.3	3.3	4.7	0.8	2.8
Turkey	5.8	4.1	2.3	3.2	0.6	5.9	2.4	1.3	1.3	12.6	56.7	7.3	7.7	22.6	61.4	11.8
Lebanon	2.0	2.3	1.2	6.8	15.5	14.1	12.4	7.6	76.5	69.8	50.6	16.2	94.0	86.2	64.3	30.6
Morocco	0.1	1.1	3.4	1.5	0.3	0.2	0.1	0.2	2.9	1.8	6.0	2.8	3.3	3.1	9.5	4.4
Tunisia	0.1	1.3	1.8	2.0	1.0	0.1	0.5	0.5	7.2	7.5	7.2	6.6	8.2	8.9	9.5	9.1
Jordan	25.0	5.5	2.6	9.8	0.1	4.9	1.2	3.4	57.3	65.5	50.1	42.7	82.5	75.9	53.9	55.9
Egypt	3.4	3.5	0.6	9.0	0.6	1.3	0.3	0.6	3.7	8.0	2.3	6.4	7.7	12.9	3.2	15.9
Bahrain	21.3	0.0	0.3	1.2	0.4	0.0	0.4	1.3	33.5	16.9	27.4	5.1	55.2	16.9	28.1	7.7
Syria	29.6	5.6	2.5	22.9	6.4	6.6	1.5	3.0	13.3	12.9	7.4	11.2	49.2	25.2	11.4	37.2
Oman	0.0	0.0	0.0	0.0	0.0	0.5	0.2	0.3	10.6	0.4	1.0	14.8	10.6	0.9	1.2	15.1
UAE	0.0	0.0	0.5	0.2	0.5	0.3	0.2	0.3	19.1	2.2	5.5	6.7	19.6	2.5	6.3	7.2
Iraq	3.6	3.8	11.5	5.3	0.3	0.2	1.8	15.9	5.8	1.6	0.2	0.0	9.6	5.7	13.5	21.1
Iran	1.7	2.3	9.1	3.8	0.1	0.1	0.0	0.1	6.8	0.6	5.8	0.7	8.6	2.9	14.9	4.5
Yemen	0.0	0.0	0.0	0.0	1.0	0.4	0.1	0.5	55.1	35.4	12.9	0.3	56.1	35.7	13.0	0.8
Saudi Arabia	2.5	0.7	2.6	2.7	4.5	2.7	6.3	1.3	1.3	0.9	0.5	3.2	8.3	4.4	9.4	7.2
Qatar	9.9	0.0	0.1	0.3	4.0	0.2	0.3	0.3	6.2	1.0	3.7	0.7	20.2	1.2	4.2	1.3
Algeria	1.3	0.0	2.3	6.4	0.3	0.0	0.0	0.0	0.2	0.0	0.1	1.9	1.9	0.1	2.5	8.3
Libya	0.7	2.6	5.9	8.4	1.0	0.0	0.0	0.7	0.2	0.1	2.8	0.4	2.0	2.8	8.6	9.5
Kuwait	0.2	0.3	1.6	1.5	1.7	0.5	0.9	0.2	4.8	3.3	3.1	1.7	6.7	4.1	5.7	3.4
Yemen, DR	0.5	0.0	0.0	—	0.3	0.1	0.0	—	9.8	59.4	0.8	—	10.6	59.5	0.8	—

Excluding oil

Israel	2.2	0.2	0.6	1.1	0.0	0.0	0.1	0.3	1.8	3.0	0.0	1.4	3.9	3.2	0.7	2.7
Turkey	4.3	4.1	2.7	3.2	0.5	5.9	3.0	1.3	1.3	12.6	69.6	7.3	6.1	22.6	75.2	11.8
Lebanon	1.0	1.6	1.2	6.9	8.3	14.2	12.4	7.7	49.7	70.5	50.6	16.4	58.9	86.3	64.3	31.0
Morocco	0.1	1.0	3.1	1.3	0.2	0.2	0.1	0.2	2.4	1.8	6.1	2.8	2.7	3.0	9.3	4.2
Tunisia	0.0	1.9	2.6	2.0	0.7	0.1	0.7	0.6	6.4	11.0	10.4	7.2	7.2	13.1	13.6	9.8
Jordan	17.4	5.5	2.8	9.8	0.1	4.9	1.3	3.4	40.2	65.5	54.5	42.7	57.7	75.9	58.6	55.9
Egypt	5.4	5.7	1.6	6.0	1.1	3.5	1.2	1.1	6.1	19.3	10.7	11.8	12.6	28.5	13.6	19.0
Bahrain	0.0	0.0	1.1	2.0	0.6	0.0	1.4	2.0	74.4	33.6	36.2	6.5	75.0	33.7	38.6	10.5
Syria	55.1	3.6	4.3	28.7	10.5	19.5	6.5	10.4	25.7	38.5	31.8	31.5	91.3	61.6	42.6	70.6
Oman	0.0	0.0	0.0	0.0	0.0	11.3	4.2	0.3	70.5	10.1	30.0	15.0	70.5	21.4	34.2	15.3
UAE	0.0	0.0	0.4	0.6	0.0	9.6	2.4	1.1	26.7	59.7	59.4	29.3	26.7	69.2	62.2	31.0
Iraq	7.9	1.0	2.1	0.5	2.8	17.0	18.0	27.0	36.6	11.5	11.5	0.1	47.4	29.6	31.6	27.5
Iran	1.6	0.8	2.6	3.4	0.2	1.1	0.9	0.5	8.4	8.4	15.4	4.5	10.2	10.2	18.9	8.4
Yemen	0.0	0.0	0.0	0.7	1.3	0.4	0.2	7.9	40.2	39.8	40.6	6.9	41.4	40.2	40.8	15.4
Saudi Arabia	19.4	0.6	2.5	3.8	56.6	10.9	5.6	8.9	9.7	33.4	5.0	24.0	85.7	44.8	13.1	36.7
Qatar	1.5	0.0	1.4	1.5	0.0	5.6	3.7	2.5	62.1	25.0	41.9	6.3	63.6	30.6	47.1	10.3
Algeria	1.4	0.6	6.2	16.9	0.3	0.4	0.0	0.1	0.3	1.0	0.1	9.7	1.9	2.0	6.3	26.7
Libya	1.2	1.7	14.2	16.9	1.8	5.1	0.1	10.6	11.6	1.5	1.1	3.7	14.6	8.3	15.3	31.3
Kuwait	4.1	5.5	0.3	5.3	25.4	11.9	7.2	4.0	57.1	56.7	35.9	41.5	86.5	74.1	43.4	50.8
Yemen, DR	1.0	0.0	0.0	—	0.8	0.2	0.1	—	32.9	83.7	6.6	—	34.7	83.8	6.7	—

Source: See table 6A-1.

References

Al-Atrash, Hassan, and Tarik Yousef. 2000. "Intra-Arab Trade: Is It Too Little?" IMF Working Paper 00/10. Washington: International Monetary Fund (January).

Cassing, Jim, and others. 2000. "Enhancing Egypt's Exports." In *Catching Up with the Competition: Trade Opportunities and Challenges for Arab Countries*, edited by Bernard Hoekman and Jamel Zarrouk. University of Michigan Press.

Chang, Won. 2000. "A Gravity Model Assessment of Intra-MENA Trade." Mimeo. World Bank.

Economic Research Forum for the Arab Countries, Iran, and Turkey (ERF). 2001. *Economic Trends in the MENA Region: 2000*. Cairo.

Francois, Joe, and Ian Wooton. 2000. "Trade in International Transport Services: The Role of Competition." *Review of International Economics* 9 (2): 249–61.

Galal, Ahmed. 2000. "Incentives for Economic Integration in the Middle East." In *Trade Policy Developments in the Middle East and North Africa*, edited by Bernard Hoekman and Hanaa Kheir-El-Din. Washington: World Bank.

Hoekman, Bernard, and Patrick Messerlin. 2000. "Liberalizing Trade in Services: Reciprocal Negotiations and Regulatory Reform." In *Services 2000: New Directions in Services Trade Liberalization*, edited by Pierre Sauvé and Robert Stern. Brookings.

———. 2002. *Harnessing Trade for Development and Growth in the Middle East and North Africa*. New York: Council on Foreign Relations.

Hoekman, Bernard, and Petros C. Mavroidis. 2000. "WTO Dispute Settlement, Transparency, and Surveillance." *World Economy* 23: 527–42.

Konan, Denise, and Keith Maskus. 2002. "Quantifying the Impact of Services Liberalization in a Developing Economy." University of Hawaii.

Mansfield, Edward. 1994. *Power, Trade, and War*. Princeton University Press.

Markusen, James, Thomas Rutherford, and David Tarr. 2002. "Foreign Direct Investment in Services and the Domestic Market for Expertise." Policy Research Working Paper 2413. Washington: World Bank.

Mattoo, Aaditya, and Carsten Fink. 2002. "Regional Agreements and Trade in Services: Policy Issues." Policy Research Working Paper 2852. Washington: World Bank.

Messerlin, Patrick. 2001. *Measuring the Costs of Protection in Europe*. Washington: Institute for International Economics.

Milward, Alan. 1984. *The Reconstruction of Western Europe, 1945–51*. London: Methuen.

———. 1992. *The European Rescue of the Nation State*. University of California Press.

Schiff, Maurice. 1996. "South-North Migration and Trade: A Survey." Policy Research Working Paper 1696. Washington: World Bank (December).

Vogel, David. 1995. *Trading Up: Consumer and Environmental Regulation in a Global Economy*. Harvard University Press.

World Bank. 2000. *Trade Blocs*. Washington.

Zarrouk, Jamel. 2000. "The Greater Arab Free Trade Area: Limits and Possibilities." In *Catching Up with the Competition: Trade Opportunities and Challenges for Arab Countries*, edited by Bernard Hoekman and Jamel Zarrouk. University of Michigan Press.

7

What Can Arab Countries Learn from Europe? An Institutional Analysis

L. ALAN WINTERS

A s Arab countries consider what economic integration may do for them and how to manage it, they naturally look for guidance from Europe, which has undergone the deepest integration, outside nation building, ever experienced.

A Brief History of European Integration

The origins of post–World War II European institutions are quite ancient, but they were given a great boost by the spirit of internationalism that pervaded the Allies' thinking about the post-war world. That internationalism gave rise to global institutions such as the International Monetary Fund and the General Agreement on Tariffs and Trade (GATT), and it also sowed the seeds for the gradual integration of the European economies and nations. European integration was essentially a political-ideological phenomenon, driven not by the careful calculation of economic costs and benefits but by a grand vision that had fortunate economic side effects.

The first major step toward economic integration was the formation in 1951 of the European Coal and Steel Community (ECSC), the origins of which were more political than economic. The members were the so-called Six—Belgium, France, West Germany, Italy, Luxembourg, and the Netherlands. The purpose of the ECSC was to stimulate the recovery of heavy industries in West Germany while making it impossible for their output ever to be used to wage war again. The proposal, developed by Jean Monnet and Robert Schuman, was that by establishing a truly common European market in coal, iron, and steel, countries would become so interdependent that war would be not only "unthinkable, but materially impossible." The common market was to be supplemented by a High Authority, which had the power to dictate national output quotas, establish maximum and minimum prices, and enforce the law of free competition (which outlawed subsidies and so forth). The High Authority was an administrative body whose policies but not day-to-day operations were controlled by the Council of the Community, on which the separate governments were represented, and by the European Parliament. The Court of Justice was established to oversee the legal affairs of the community.

Subsequent attempts were made to establish further supranational European organizations. A defense community and a political community were negotiated among the Six, but they foundered, mainly on the rock of French politics. Then in 1955 plans were made to form a general common market—the European Economic Community (EEC)—and an atomic energy community, Euratom. Those plans came to fruition in the Treaty of Rome in 1957, after a period of intense negotiation. At first, the EEC and Euratom existed separately but parallel to the ECSC, but in 1967 the three bodies were merged, with one commission (successor to the High Authority), one council, one parliament, and one court. Together they constituted the European Communities (EC), which has more recently evolved into the European Union (EU).[1]

This chapter briefly surveys the history and internal organization of European integration. Few of the chapter's propositions can be rigorously tested, but they do have a ring of plausibility. However, one of the lessons that can be drawn from the European experience is that integration should

---

1. The precise terminology for the group of members has varied through time and by subject matter—for example, trade policy is still formally the preserve of the European Community within the European Union. European Union (EU) is used as the general-purpose phrase.

be thought of as a whole and as a process, rather than as a series of separate steps that can be undertaken and analyzed in isolation.[2]

A European Separation of Powers

The current institutions of European integration clearly reflect those of the ECSC more than fifty years ago.[3] The European Commission now comprises twenty commissioners appointed by member states for four-year terms, two from each of the larger members and one from the others. It initiates community policy and executes it, but it cannot actually make policy; that falls to the European Council. The commission is explicitly supranational, charged with preserving and promoting the European ideal. It represents the EU as a body in world trade negotiations, and it is acquiring a role in other forums such as the OECD and World Summit (G-7) meetings.

The European Council formally comprises the foreign ministers of all member states, although most business is conducted by deputies—either the ministers concerned with specific issues (for example, agriculture ministers discuss the common agricultural policy (CAP) and finance ministers the budget) or, for day-to-day matters, permanent officials.[4] The council shares executive power with the commission. It may adopt the commission's policy proposals, in which case they become law, but generally it may not amend them. Decisions theoretically are taken by qualified majority vote (at least 62 of 87 votes); votes are allocated to member states according to size. Until recently, however, a country had right of veto on important issues of national interest; as a result, most decisions were reached by trading compromises on often unrelated issues to obtain a unanimously acceptable package. Recent changes have reestablished majority voting in most spheres, and it is hoped that this will reduce the horse-trading.

The European Court of Justice interprets community law, and its findings are binding even on member governments. The judges are appointed by member states; however, they are required to be independent of national interests and they cannot be removed by member governments.

2 This chapter draws on Winters (1997).

3. Molle (2001) gives more detail of EU institutions.

4. The meeting of heads of government is known as the European Council. It has regular, biannual meetings.

The European Parliament has a small but growing role in the EU. It must be consulted by the commission and the council before they decide many issues, and it has some power over the community budget. Its greatest power is the ability to dismiss the European Commission en masse, although this weapon is so unwieldy that it is of little practical use.

Managing Spillovers and Enlargement

Britain did nothing to hinder integration among the Six, but it was reluctant to join anything smacking of supranationality or federalism. It felt different from the other European countries, with stronger ties with America and the rest of the world and also with a much smaller and more efficient agricultural sector. Therefore, while Britain favored intra-European free trade, it resisted the administrative and political structures of the EEC. The Scandinavian countries had similar suspicions, while the Swiss constitution explicitly forbade the government to join international political associations such as the EEC, and the Eastern European powers objected to Austria joining. These countries therefore excluded themselves from the EEC and, fearful that they would suffer as the EEC stimulated the competitiveness of the Six, formed a looser association in 1960—the European Free Trade Association (EFTA)—to promote free trade in manufactures among themselves. The members were Austria, Denmark, Norway, Portugal, Sweden, Switzerland, and the UK; of the members, the UK was entirely dominant.

Very soon after EFTA was initiated, however, the UK changed its mind and sought full membership of the EEC. Negotiations took more than a decade, with agreement reached in 1971 for accession in 1973. Ireland and Denmark reached similar agreements, because once Britain decided to join they had virtually no choice. Their agricultural exports to the UK, which were substantial, would have been decimated if they had stayed outside.

The terms of accession were not very favorable to the new members, reflecting the acquis communitaire, the EU convention—probably correct from the point of view of political practicality—that new members have to accept all community practices as they stand at the time of accession. The first enlargement showed that integration does have regional spillover effects. For large neighbors they are largely political demonstration effects; for smaller countries, the economic consequences probably predominate. The economic aspect was evident in the subsequent enlargements to Greece,

Iberia, Scandinavia, and Austria, all of which were essentially economic on the accedants' part and political on the part of the EU.[5] The current enlargement to central and eastern Europe illustrates the same phenomenon, although with the addition of political (security) motives for the accedants.

One feature of all enlargements has been the use of long transition periods in sensitive areas to ease the transition to full membership, on both sides of the bargain. A long period essentially decouples the institutional commitment from the stress of adjustment, postponing much of the stress until the commitment looks more or less indisputable.[6] There appears to be something irreversible about accession to the EU, for despite periodic rumblings among the electorates of member states, continuing membership has always been the establishment's position, usually with strong multiparty support. That support is arguably due to the fact that the day-to-day business of running the EU, with its multilateral contact and cooperation, binds politicians and bureaucrats strongly to European institutions.

Internal Transfers

A second feature, thrown into relief by the southern accession—comprising Greece in 1981 and Spain and Portugal in 1986—is distribution. The willingness of the incumbents to make budgetary transfers to the southern accedants clearly smoothed their entry path. Whether it was essential, however, is difficult to tell, for the transfers were not the only perceived long-term benefit to the new members. It is reasonable to argue, however, that the transfer mechanism—small as it is compared with those in federal and unitary states—has been essential to running the EU since the southern accession occurred. In fact, distribution is a major factor in all EU decisionmaking. The existence of institutions to address it prevents it from becoming an impassable barrier to progress and reduces the scope for distributional issues to disturb efficiency decisions. Transfers quite clearly are one of the forms of specie in political trading within the EU.

Keeping the Flame Alight

European integration has always been a rather off-and-on affair, with periods of enthusiasm and rapid advancement followed by periods of doubt,

---

5. See, in particular, Baldwin (1995, 1997) and Baldwin, Forslid, and Haaland (1996).
6. Of course, adjustment might actually entail lower absolute cost if it is spread over a long period or postponed, but it correspondingly postpones the benefits as well.

retrenchment, and even reverse. Understandably, the former are associated with economic booms and the latter with recessions. Thus the early 1980s found the EU very much down in the dumps. After the severe anti-inflationary policies at the beginning of the decade, the U.S. and Japanese economies began to recover, but the economies of the EU seemed firmly stuck in the mire. Moreover, the rapid increase in intra-EU trade that had characterized the early stages of integration seemed to be reversing. Doubts were expressed about even the viability of the EU as an institution, let alone any further progress.

During such depressions, the European Commission's role as guardian and champion of the European ideal has been vital to the goal of integration. While member governments are focusing on their local problems, the commission is required to take a broader, longer, and more European view. In the mid-1980s its response to the lethargy of the European economy was dramatic and imaginative, but subtly balanced and well directed at the same time. It had long been recognized that the actual integration of the EU economies fell short of the aspirations of the Treaty of Rome, and with the increasing focus on national policy and political difficulties, there were signs that it was reversing. Recalling the stimulus that the initial creation of the EEC had induced and following the prevailing trend toward economic liberalism, the European Commission pressed the case for a bold step toward complete economic integration. The new Single European Act provided the political framework, while the economic and legislative program was defined in a white paper.[7] The political skill with which the fractious and self-absorbed member governments were led to subscribe to such dramatic economic reform was of the highest order. The process of completion clearly involved a shift of sovereignty from national governments toward EU institutions, and yet it achieved sufficient momentum to carry along even the most doubtful of governments.

Completing the European internal market primarily entailed confirming the "four freedoms of movement" within the EU defined in the Treaty of Rome: movement of goods, services, capital, and persons. Broadly speaking, in 1985 the remaining barriers to movement and hence to the reform agenda for the Single Market Program were the following: restrictions on market access (through, for instance, customs formalities between EU

7. Commission of the European Communities (1985).

member states); different national technical standards and foreign exchange controls; distortions of competitive conditions (through, for instance, state subsidies, biased public purchasing, merger regulations, and the airline cartel); and different national approaches to market functioning (as in, for example, indirect taxes, trademarks, company law, the prudential regulation of banks, and professional qualifications). The first two sets of barriers were to be crossed by eliminating the offending practices. Dealing with the third set entailed harmonizing national regulations, although it also frequently entailed liberalization—that is, less restrictive or interventionary harmonizing—through member states' recognition of each other's regulations and competition between national rules rather than the imposition of common regulations by Brussels. The white paper contains at least two imaginative approaches to integration. First it gives primacy to the question of market access. Once free market access is ensured, it becomes much more difficult and expensive for governments to pursue other distortionary policies because those policies can be undermined by international trade. If, for example, imports are allowed to move into a domestic market, the government finds it much harder to justify shackling its own firms with excessive regulation.

Second, overcoming the tendency to write regulations centrally was highly significant: mutual recognition of each others' regulations is much less threatening to national authorities than is "interference by Brussels," even though it often entails much the same outcome. Mutual recognition has not been wholly effective in removing standards-related trade barriers, but it has at least helped.

Realistic Expectations and Pragmatic Enforcement

As the patchy progress toward the single European market illustrates, European integration has continued and survived because its advocates have been realistic about what can be achieved. Compromise and pragmatism have been the watchwords, and although the outcome is messy and frequently second-best in economic terms, European integration has manifestly avoided collapse or even serious regression. Its endurance has been due in major part to voting rules that make it difficult for the majority to impose policies on the minority. But beyond that, the "grand vision" has rendered the survival of the integration process more important than the details, leading to great sensitivity about confronting fundamental national interests. Therefore members in reality have strong veto rights, even if formally majority voting applies. Third, the commission is very sensitive in enforcing EU law. All members are in violation of some directives and regulations, and yet such cases rarely end up in the Court of Justice. (When they do, there are fewer compromises.) In addition, in several instances exceptions and derogations from legislation have been granted.

Policymaking for a Common Market

This section deals with two aspects of policymaking within the EU that contain serious lessons for other blocs. The first concerns the design of common implementing institutions. The second concerns the design of the regional "constitution."

Institutions for Trade Policymaking

A newly formed customs union fixes its external tariff in negotiation, but it still needs a means for determining changes in that tariff. European integration has proceeded alongside a gradual liberalization of the EU's manufactures trade with the rest of the world, which has reduced the degree of trade diversion, enhanced external trade creation, and stimulated competition within the customs union. One must ask, however, whether external liberalization has proceeded as smoothly as it might have and how the EU has come to persist with such an inefficient agricultural trade policy. Even on trade liberalization there are lessons to be learned.[8]

The first of these lessons concerns the difficulties of making policy through committees of representatives, especially if, as in the EU, ultimate responsibility for the outcome is diffuse or confused. As noted above, the separation of powers within the EU allows (requires) the European Commission to propose and the council to dispose policy. The council has the power to amend commission proposals and to sack the commission if it can do so unanimously, but otherwise it has, roughly speaking, only the power to accept or reject commission policies. That would appear to give the commission considerable power to determine the future of the EU, but, in fact, despite the many complaints from national capitals about the loss of national sovereignty, that is not really the case. Rejecting a European Commission

8. Winters (1995) discusses many of these issues in a different context.

proposal merely leaves the status quo in place, and rejecting a trade policy requires only a minority of council votes or, where vital national interests are alleged to be at stake, only one.

The status quo is usually fine for national politicians jealous of their national power, but it leaves the commission impotent. Hence if the commission is to achieve anything, it must broker compromises between national governments. Moreover, nearly the whole of the EU trade policy process is undertaken by bureaucrats of one sort or another. Messerlin notes that bureaucrats have a penchant for secrecy and also a strong interest in excessive and complex protection schemes if they are unable to reap any of the surpluses their policies create. In this regard the EU's procedures are quite unlike the processes of the United States, in which everything is so public.[9]

This decisionmaking structure tends to lead the EU toward protectionist outcomes. The compromises and bargaining may avoid extreme forms of capture by national interests, but it encourages a drift toward generalized protection and strengthens the hand of EU-wide lobbies that can bring pressure to bear not only in Brussels but also in national capitals—for example, the agriculture lobby and the iron and steel lobbies.

The best known policymaking failure deriving from the EU's committee approach is the "restaurant bill" problem afflicting the agricultural council's annual price-fixing exercises. The costs of high agricultural prices are born by consumers and—of much greater significance to policymakers—the EU budget. The benefits are more or less proportional to production. Because the marginal euro of the EU budget is levied per unit of GDP, each national government has an incentive to seek price rises in any commodity for which its share of EU production exceeds its share of GDP. Nearly every country has some such candidates. Moreover, all national governments have some degree of trouble from their lobbies, and the EU-wide farm lobby is very keen to see the benefits of support spread widely across their membership. Hence all the political incentives are for widespread agricultural price increases.

In agriculture, we need no further explanation of why the EU raises internal prices and hence external protection, but development of the restaurant bill model helps to explain the tendency toward protection in

9. Messerlin (1983).

industry. It arises from the difficulty of making the following argument in a plausible and principled fashion: "We oppose this measure as harmful to EU interests, but if you persist with it we want a share of the benefits." It is the tendency toward universalism discussed by Shepsle and Weingast.[10]

Universalism is the phenomenon whereby policy packages emerge in which everyone receives some "favor" even though, in sum, the favors detract from welfare. It gives rise to policy packages of protection in which each partner prefers to be on the inside (that is, protected) than on the outside, even though each might oppose protection in principle. Therefore, if the protection of, say, certain parts of the steel industry is being considered, member governments seek to extend protection to those parts of the industry in which they have a large interest as the price for their cooperation. They may do so even if their best outcome would be that the steel industry were not protected at all; that is because the worst outcome is to have an unprotected part of a protected industry, and they are unsure of their ability to block protection in total. A historical example is seen in British ministers' discussions of Agriculture Commissioner MacSharry's (barely adequate) reforms to the common agricultural policy in 1992, when they gave higher priority to ensuring that large farms were eligible for generous set-aside compensation payments than to their professed fundamental aim of reducing the payments themselves. Better to have the British big-farm sector inside the deal than outside if it passed despite British opposition.

Another dimension of bias toward protectionism is evident in the tussle over trade policy among different parts of government. This is well illustrated by the EU's experience with nontariff barriers on trade with nonmember countries. These are dealt with only under the rather nonspecific economic policy section of the Treaty of Rome, and for many years it was not clear whether the central EU or the national authorities controlled them. Over time the central authorities have prevailed, but at the expense of adopting certain protectionist policies that particular national governments wished to impose. For example, in 1988 the French and Italians sought protection from Korean and Taiwanese footwear imports, and they were allowed to introduce national voluntary export restraints—an instance of the EU authorities essentially introducing national trade policies despite their declared mission to abolish such things in the name of the single European

10. Shepsle and Weingast (1981).

market. That embarrassment was soon overcome, however, by extending the policy to the whole of EU imports from Korea and Taiwan. In order to capture and cement control over trade policy, the European Commission has adopted policies based on those of the more protectionist members and propagated them over the whole EU, albeit in somewhat diluted fashion.

One lesson that could be drawn from trade policymaking in the EU is that responsibility for trade policy and all its outcomes should be clearly lodged in a single entity, ideally an executive subject to broad periodic guidance and review by elected legislatures. To the maximum extent possible, committees of national bureaucrats, whose horizons are necessarily limited, should be avoided.

Constitutional Policies

If the objective of a regional arrangement is deep integration, common policies may well be useful. However, the European experience of enshrining them in the constitution is salutary. The Treaties of Paris and Rome obliged the EU to pursue common policies in three sectors: agriculture, transport, and energy, and the structures of the European Coal and Steel Community were designed, in keeping with the interventionism of the early 1950s, to facilitate both price and production controls. Production controls have since been used extensively to support the coal sector, leaving it one of the most distorted sectors in the 1980s, and the situation in steel was little better during this period.

Agriculture provides the most salutary lessons, however. It was a key sector in the post-war European economies, and it was heavily supported by national governments. A common policy was required to ensure that national differences in support did not distort competition in the common market, and naturally it was very interventionist. Price support policies for supply-elastic goods contain the seeds of their own demise, but in the EU it was trebly difficult to control them. First, the common agricultural policy established a new bureaucracy, and for many years it was the most tangible of Brussels's bureaucratic achievements. Second, the administrative structure of the CAP was deeply flawed—see the details of its price-setting procedures described previously. And third, the "need" for agricultural intervention was enshrined in the Treaty of Rome—essentially the EU's constitution—making it extraordinarily difficult to tackle through the business of ordinary politics.

Explicit mention in the treaty—especially of any policy prescriptions—legitimizes one particular constellation of policies, affirming a "right" to the benefits it provides. The absence of an exit mechanism, coupled with the EU's pragmatic bargaining approach to policymaking, puts huge pressure on member governments to reach an agreement of some sort. And because change requires near unanimity, a legitimized status quo becomes a very likely outcome in any policy debate.[11] Moreover, under such circumstances any change negotiated tends to be an agglomeration of specific provisions catering to the various interests represented in the decisionmaking body, reinforcing the restaurant bill and universalist effects already noted: because EU decisionmaking bodies comprise the representatives of national governments rather than of legislatures or electorates, bureaucratic interests receive a very high weight in the process. The result is that reform becomes almost impossible except in deep crises that make maintaining the status quo infeasible.

Conclusion

This chapter has attempted to extract some lessons for Arab economic integration from the European experience—the strongest example to date of economic integration other than nation building. In conclusion, those lessons are presented in the order of their estimated strategic importance for Arab countries seeking to generate more rather than less economic welfare from their integration arrangements.

Constitutional Design

The lessons related to constitutional design concern the fundamental need for strong political backing for integration and for some sort of central executive body.

—European integration was essentially a political-ideological phenomenon. It was not driven by the careful calculation of economic costs and benefits, but by a grand vision that had fortunate economic side effects.

—During depressions, the European Commission's role as the guardian and champion of the European ideal has been vital to maintaining and advancing integration.

11. See Scharpf (1988).

—If a choice is made to pursue a customs union (a common external trade policy), responsibility for trade policy and all its outcomes should be clearly lodged in a single entity—an executive subject to broad periodic guidance and review from elected legislatures.

—It is dangerous to give particular sectors special constitutional standing or their own bureaucracy. Each makes reform very difficult even when circumstances have changed radically.

—Integration has regional spillover effects, generally political demonstration effects for large neighbors and economic consequences for smaller ones.

Political Operations

Lessons relating to political operations concern intermediate political objectives—factors that help integration along regardless of how institutions are designed. They highlight the need for pragmatism and realism if integration is to avoid the strains of constant evaluation and challenge.

—Be realistic about what integration will achieve.

—Distribution is a major factor in EU decisionmaking, but the existence of institutions to address it prevents it from becoming an impassable barrier to progress and reduces the scope for distributional issues to disturb efficiency decisions.

—Resist the urge to write regulations: mutual recognition is much less threatening to national authorities than is "interference by Brussels," even though it often entails much the same outcome.

—Long transition periods ease the process of transition to full membership on both sides of the bargain. They essentially decouple the institutional commitment from the stress of adjustment, postponing much of the stress until the commitment looks more or less indisputable.

—In devising policies for deep integration, give primacy to the question of market access.

References

Baldwin, R. E. 1995. "A Domino Theory of Regionalism." In *Expanding Membership in the European Union*, edited by R. E. Baldwin, P. Haapranta, and J. Kiander, 25–48. Cambridge University Press.

————. 1997. "The Causes of Regionalism." *World Economy* 20: 865–88.

Baldwin, R. E., R. Forslid, and J. I. Haaland. 1996. "Investment Creation and Diversion in Europe." *World-Economy* 19 (6): 635–59.

Commission of the European Communities. 1985. "Completing the Internal Market." *Com* 85: 310.

Messerlin, P. A. 1983. "Bureaucracies and the Political Economy of Protection: Reflections of a Continental European." *Weltwirtschaftliches Archiv* 117: 461–96.

Molle, W. 2001. *The Economics of European Integration*. Burlington, Vt.: Ashgate.

Scharpf, F. W. 1988. "The Joint-Decision Trap: Lessons from German Federalism and European Integration." *Public Administration* 66: 239–78.

Shepsle, K. A., and B. R. Weingast. 1981. "Political Preferences for the Pork Barrel: A Generalization." *American Journal of Political Science* 25: 96–111.

Winters, L. A., ed. 1995. *Foundations of an Open Economy*. London: Center for Economic Policy Research.

———. 1997. "What Is European Experience Teaching Developing Countries about Integration?" *World Economy* 20: 889–912.

Contributors

Samiha Fawzy
*Egyptian Center for Economic
Studies*

Ahmed Galal
*Egyptian Center for Economic
Studies*

Bernard Hoekman
*World Bank and Centre for
Economic Policy Research*

Denise Eby Konan
University of Hawaii

Patrick Messerlin
Institut d'Etudes Politiques de Paris

L. Alan Winters
*University of Sussex and Center for
Economic Policy Research*

Jamel Zarrouk
*Arab Monetary Fund and Economic
Research Forum for the Arab
Countries, Iran, and Turkey*

Index